VOGUE® KNITTING

CROCHETED
BABY BLANKETS

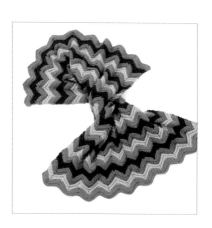

VOGUE® KNITTING

CROCHETED
BABY BLANKETS

SIXTH&SPRING BOOKS
NEW YORK

SIXTH&SPRING BOOKS
233 Spring Street
New York, New York 10013

Resource information is current at time of publication.
We have made every effort to ensure the accuracy of the contents of this publication.
We are not responsible for any human or typographical errors.

Library of Congress Cataloging-in-Publication Data

Library of Congress Control Number: 2006931205
ISBN: 1-933027-10-X
ISBN-13: 978-1-933027-10-4

Manufactured in China

1 3 5 7 9 10 8 6 4 2

First Edition
2007

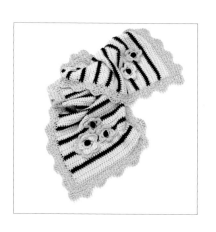

TABLE OF CONTENTS

18 **SHELL STITCH BLANKET**
Cherry lemonade

20 **RIPPLE BLANKET**
Nautical and nice

22 **ZIGZAG BLANKET**
Crazy crayons

25 **TRELLIS BLANKET**
Lavender lullaby

28 **FLORAL BLANKET**
Salt water taffy

31 **DUCK BLANKET**
Ducks in a row

36 **AMISH-STYLE BLANKET**
Star quality

40 **MEDALLION BLANKET**
Garden variety

45 **RELIEF STITCH BLANKET**
Hydrangea bouquet

48 **LACE BLANKET**
Pistachio parfait

54 **BUNDLER BLANKET**
Pretty papoose

58 **BUNNY BLANKET**
Hop to it

62 **GRANNY SQUARE BLANKET**
Lucky charms

65 **FLORAL MEDALLION BLANKET**
Pumpkin spice

68 **SHELLS BLANKET**
Zebra Z's

71 **CLOVER BLANKET**
Blues snooze

74 **SQUARE MEDALLION BLANKET**
Squaring the circle

77 **WOVEN BLANKET**
Green piece

80 **STARS AND MOONS BLANKET**
Twinkle, twinkle

84 **TRADITIONAL GRANNY BLANKET**
Petunia patchwork

87 **GEOMETRIC BLANKET**
Boho beauty

90 **EYELET BLANKET**
Lilac luxe

92 **PATCHWORK SAMPLER**
Sleeping spumoni

97 **CABLED BLANKET**
Orange you sleepy?

INTRODUCTION

Crocheting a baby blanket is a wonderful, personal way to commemorate a baby's birth. How many of us still cherish the precious pieces made by hand and given to us when we were young? Crocheting a blanket allows us to pass that same special feeling on to our loved ones as they start their journey through life.

Compact in size, baby blankets require a minimum investment of time to yield gorgeous results. In *Vogue Knitting On the Go! Crocheted Baby Blankets* you will find twenty-four patterns for beautiful blankets no matter how experienced you are with a hook and yarn. You will find a multitude of traditional designs, such as the Granny Square Blanket on p. 62, the Zigzag Blanket on p. 22, and the Shell Stitch Blanket on p. 18; adorable pictorals, such as the Stars and Moons Blanket on p. 80 and the Duck Blanket on p. 31; and more challenging patterns such as the Cabled Blanket on p. 97.

The birth of a baby is cause for celebration, and the joy that goes into making a blanket will stay with its recipient for a lifetime. Congratulations on the newborn in your life—and get ready to crochet **ON THE GO!**

THE BASICS

Delicate heirloom or heavy-duty crib warmer, a crocheted baby blanket is a treasured gift and a fuss-free project that will last a lifetime. Crocheted baby blankets are perfectly suited for crocheters who are just starting out, or who are experienced and want to move their skills to the next level. Some feature squares or strips that are later assembled during finishing; others, made in one piece, require little more than the simplest stitches; still others offer crocheted lace, cables and delicate appliqués to spice things up. Many of the designs are quick and easy, and baby blankets by nature are portable, so taking your crocheting "on the go" will be no problem at all.

All the designs in this book can be altered in size to make them larger or smaller. To adjust most patterns, you can use the traditional method of increasing or decreasing the number of stitches and rows, as well as add or subtract squares, to achieve the desired size. You can also change the yarn weight and/or needle size to create a custom-sized blanket. Remember to adjust yarn requirements and the number of stitches around the edge accordingly.

FINISHING

Since blankets are frequently crocheted in one piece, keep finishing in mind when beginning your blanket project.

1. Because the back-side of the fabric will be seen when the blanket is used, you must be ready for the reverse to be on display. Think about using a stitch that is reversible, or one that looks good on both sides, such as the one in the Zigzag Blanket on page 22.

2. When adding a new yarn, be careful to do so at a place where you can easily weave the ends in, such as the sides, as there is frequently no "wrong side" on a blanket.

3. Consider adding a fabric backing as a whimsical and practical accent to your fine handwork.

Crochet is accessible and really quite easy to learn. Stitches are formed by pulling loops through other loops, or stitches, with a hook, creating the simple chain that is used in all patterns. Unlike knitting, it requires no balancing act with needles, shifting stitches from one needle to another. In crochet, one hand and one hook do all the work, and finished fabric lays away from the hook, letting crocheters concentrate only on the next stitch they need to make. And, unlike other crafts, correcting a mistake is fairly stress-free—simply tug on the yarn to easily pull out the stitches you have worked.

GAUGE

Most blanket patterns don't rely on perfect fit as a garment does, but it is still important to crochet a gauge swatch. Measure gauge as illustrated here. (Launder and block your gauge swatch before taking measurements). Try different hook sizes until your sample measures the required number of stitches and rows. To get fewer stitches to the inch/cm, use larger hooks; to get more stitches to the inch/cm, use smaller needles. It's a good idea to keep your gauge swatch to

test any embroidery or embellishment, and blocking and cleaning methods.

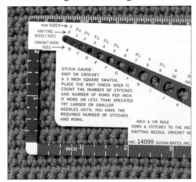

If you're not convinced that it's easy to learn to crochet, perhaps the pieces in this collection will inspire you. They run the gamut from basic to more complicated stitches, giving experienced crocheters ample challenge and offering novices the chance to graduate to more difficult projects as they progress. The beginner styles, such as the Eyelet Blanket on page

90 and the Floral Blanket on page 28, often have a simple one-row or two-row repeat and work up quickly with a very large hook and bulky-weight yarn. Such basic patterns let the yarn take center stage. Meanwhile, the more advanced designs, like the Patchwork Sampler on page 92 do not necessarily have more difficult stitch techniques; rather, the

CROCHET HOOKS					
U.S.	**Metric**	**U.S.**	**Metric**	**U.S.**	**Metric**
B/I	2.25mm	G/6	4mm	K/10.5	6.5mm
C/2	2.75mm	7	4.5mm	L/11	8mm
D/3	3.25mm	H/8	5mm	M/13	9mm
E/4	3.5mm	I/9	5.5mm	N/15	10mm
F/5	3.75mm	J/10	6mm		

instructions, with their series of repeats and pattern layouts, require more concentration to create the perfect piece.

For an exact reproduction of the blanket photographed, use the yarn listed in the materials section of the pattern. We've selected yarns that are readily available in the U.S. and Canada at the time of printing. The Resources list on page 100 provides addresses of yarn distributors. Contact them for the name of a retailer in your area.

YARN SUBSTITUTION

You may wish to substitute yarns. Perhaps a spectacular yarn matches your baby's room; maybe you view small-scale projects as a chance to incorporate leftovers from your yarn stash; or it may be that the yarn specified is not available in your area. Blankets allow you to be as creative as you like, but you'll need to crochet to the given gauge to obtain the finished measurements with the substitute yarn. Make pattern adjustments where necessary. Be sure to consider how different yarn types (chenille, mohair, bouclé, etc.) will affect the final appearance of your blanket, and how they will feel against a baby's skin. Also take fiber care into consideration: Some yarns can be machine- or hand-washed; others will require dry cleaning.

To facilitate yarn substitution, *Vogue Knitting* grades yarn by the standard stitch gauge obtained in single crochet. You'll find a grading number in the "Materials" section of the pattern immediately following the yarn information. Look for a substitute yarn that falls into the same category. The suggested hook size and gauge on the ball band should be comparable to that on the Standard Yarn Weight chart at right.

After you've successfully gauge-swatched a substitute yarn, you'll need to determine how much of the substitute yarn the project requires. First, find the total yardage of the original yarn in the pattern (multiply the number of balls by yards/meters per ball). Divide this figure by the new yards/meters per ball (listed on the ball band). Round up to the next whole number. The result is the number of balls required.

READING CROCHET INSTRUCTIONS

If you are used to reading knitting instructions, then crochet instructions may seem a little tedious to follow. Crochet instructions use more abbreviations and punctuation and fewer words than traditional knitting instructions. Along with the separation of stitches and use of brackets, parentheses, commas and other punctuation, numerous repetitions may

Categories of yarn, gauge ranges, and recommended needle and hook sizes

Yarn Weight Symbol & Category Names	(1) Super Fine	(2) Fine	(3) Light	(4) Medium	(5) Bulky	(6) Super Bulky
Type of Yarns in Category	Sock, Fingering, Baby	Sport, Baby	DK, Light Worsted	Worsted, Afghan, Aran	Chunky, Craft, Rug	Bulky, Roving
Knit Gauge Range* in Stockinette Stitch to 4 Inches	27–32 sts	23–26 sts	21–24 sts	16–20 sts	12–15 sts	6–11 sts
Recommended Needle in Metric Size Range	2.25–3.25 mm	3.25–3.75 mm	3.75–4.5 mm	4.5–5.5 mm	5.5–8 mm	8 mm and larger
Recommended Needle U.S. Size Range	1 to 3	3 to 5	5 to 7	7 to 9	9 to 11	11 and larger
Crochet Gauge* Ranges in Single Crochet To 4 Inch	21–32 sts	16–20 sts	12–17 sts	11–14 sts	8–11 sts	5–9 sts
Recommended Hook in Metric Size Range	2.25–3.5 mm	3.5–4.5 mm	4.5–5.5 mm	5.5–6.5 mm	6.5–9 mm	9 mm and larger
Recommended Hook U.S. Size Range	B–1 to E–4	E–4 to 7	7 to I–9	I–9 to K–10½	K–10½ to M–13	M–13 and larger

*Guidelines only: The above reflects the most commonly used needle or hook sizes for specific yarn categories.

■□□□
Beginner
Ideal first project.

■■□□
Very Easy Very Vogue
Basic stitches, minimal shaping, simple finishing.

■■■□
Intermediate
For crocheters with some experience. More intricate stitches, shaping and finishing.

■■■■
Experienced
For crocheters able to work patterns with complicated shaping and finishing.

occur within a single row or round. Therefore, you must pay close attention to reading instructions while you crochet. Here are a few explanations of the more common terms used in this book.

Use of Parentheses ( )

Sometimes parentheses are used to indicate stitches that are to be worked all into one stitch, such as "in next st work ( )" or "( ) in next st."

First st, Next st

The beginning stitch of every row is referred to as the "first st." When counting the turning chain (t-ch) as 1 stitch, the row or round will begin by instructing that you work into the next st (that is, skip the first st or space or whatever is designated in the pattern).

Stitch Counts

Sometimes the turning chain that is worked at the end (or beginning) of a row or a round will be referred to as 1 stitch and is then counted in the stitch count. In those cases, you will work into the next stitch, thus skipping the first stitch of the row or round. When the turning chain is not counted as a stitch, work into the first actual stitch.

Stitches Described

Sometimes the stitches are described as sc, dc, tr, ch-2 loop, 2-dc group, etc. and sometimes—such as in a mesh pattern of sc, ch 1—each sc and each ch 1 will be referred to as a st.

Back Loop

Along the top of each crochet stitch or chain there are two loops. The loop furthest away from you is the "back loop."

Front Loop

Along the top of each crochet stitch or chain there are two loops. The loop closest to you is the "front loop."

Joining New Colors

When joining new colors in crochet, whether at the beginning of a row or while

STANDARD BLANKET SIZES

Use these measurements as a guide—you may need to adjust them to accommodate stitch and color patterns and repeats.

■ Receiving

30"–36"/76cm–91.5cm square

■ Carriage

24"–30"/61cm–76cm square
18"–24"/45.5cm–61cm wide x
24"–30"/61cm–76cm long

■ Crib

36"–42"/91.5-106.5cm square
34"–40"/86cm–101.5cm wide x
38"–44"/96.5cm–111.5cm long

■ Throw/Afghan

34"–44"/101.5cm–111.5cm wide x
38"–48"/96.5cm–122cm long

working across, always work the stitch in the old color to the last 2 loops, then draw the new color through the 2 loops and continue with the new color.

Working Over Ends

Crochet has a unique flat top along each row that is perfect for laying the old color across and working over the ends for several stitches. This will alleviate the need to cut and weave in ends later.

Form a Ring

When a pattern is worked in the round, as in a square or medallion, the beginning chains are usually closed into a ring by working a slip stitch into the first chain. Then on the first round, stitches are usually worked into the ring and less often into each chain.

BLOCKING

Blocking crochet is usually not necessary. However, in those cases when you do need to smooth out the fabric, choose a blocking method consistent with information on the yarn care label and, when in doubt, test your gauge swatch. Note that some yarns, such as chenilles and ribbons, do not benefit from blocking.

Wet Block Method

Using rustproof pins, pin scarf to measurements on a flat surface and lightly dampen using a spray bottle. Allow to dry before removing pins.

Steam Block Method

Pin scarf to measurements with wrong side of the fabric facing up. Steam lightly, holding the iron 2"/5cm above the work. Do not press the iron directly onto the piece, as it will flatten the stitches.

CARE

Refer to the yarn label for the recommended cleaning method. Many of the blankets in the book can be washed by hand (or in the machine on a gentle or wool cycle) in lukewarm water with a mild detergent. Do not agitate, and don't soak for more than 10 minutes. Rinse gently with tepid water, then fold in a towel and gently press the water out. Lay flat to dry, away from excessive heat and light.

CHAIN

I *Pass the yarn over the hook and catch it with the hook.*

2 *Draw the yarn through the loop on the hook.*

3 *Repeat steps 1 and 2 to make a chain.*

SINGLE CROCHET

I *Insert the hook through top two loops of a stitch. Pass the yarn over the hook and draw up a loop—two loops on hook.*

2 *Pass the yarn over the hook and draw through both loops on hook.*

3 *Continue in the same way, inserting the hook into each stitch.*

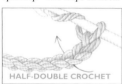

HALF-DOUBLE CROCHET

I *Pass the yarn over the hook. Insert the hook through the top two loops of a stitch.*

2 *Pass the yarn over the hook and draw up a loop—three loops on hook. Pass the yarn over the hook.*

3 *Draw through all three loops on hook.*

DOUBLE CROCHET

I *Pass the yarn over the hook. Insert the hook through the top two loops of a stitch.*

2 *Pass the yarn over the hook and draw up a loop—three loops on hook.*

SLIP STITCH

Insert the crochet hook into a stitch, catch the yarn and pull up a loop. Draw the loop through the loop on the hook.

3 *Pass the yarn over the hook and draw it through the first two loops on the hook, pass the yarn over the hook and draw through the remaining two loops. Continue in the same way, inserting the hook into each stitch.*

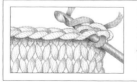

Illustrations: Joni Coniglio

CROCHET TERMS AND ABBREVIATIONS

approx approximately

beg begin(ning)

CC contrast color

ch chain(s)

cm centimeter(s)

cont continue(ing)

dc double crochet (U.K.: tr-treble)

dec decrease(ing)–Reduce the stitches in a row (work stitches together or skip the stitches).

foll follow(s)(ing)

g gram(s)

hdc half double crochet (U.K.: htr-half treble)

inc increase(ing)–Add stitches in a row (work extra stitches into a stitch or between the stitches).

LH left-hand

lp(s) loop(s)

m meter(s)

MC main color

mm millimeter(s)

oz ounce(s)

pat(s) pattern

pm place markers–Place or attach a loop of contrast yarn or purchased stitch marker as indicated.

rem remain(s)(ing)

rep repeat

rnd(s) round(s)

RH right-hand

RS right side(s)

sc single crochet (U.K.: dc-double crochet)

sk skip

sl st slip stitch (U.K.: single crochet)

sp(s) space(s)

st(s) stitch(es)

t-ch turning chain

tog together

tr treble (U.K.: tr tr-triple treble)

WS wrong side(s)

work even Continue in pattern without increasing or decreasing. (U.K.: work straight)

yd yard(s)

yo yarn over–Wrap the yarn around the hook (U.K.: yrh)

* Repeat directions following * as many times as indicated.

[ ] Repeat directions inside brackets as many times as indicated.

SHELL STITCH BLANKET

Cherry lemonade

Shells and stripes are forever in this design by Tanis Gray. There are not one, but two shell and single-crochet stitch combination patterns: one in the blanket and the other in the border.

FINISHED MEASUREMENTS
■ 22½"/57cm wide x 31½"/80cm long

MATERIALS
■ 2 4oz/113g skeins (each approx 165yds/151m) of Fiesta Yarns *Insignia La Boheme* (rayon/brushed kid mohair/wool/nylon) each in #2512 cherry tomato (A) and #2556 goldenrod (B) (⬛4⬛)
■ 2 4oz/113g skeins (each approx 210yds/192m) of Fiesta Yarns *Soccoro* (wool/nylon) in #27132 tequila sunrise (C) (⬛4⬛)
■ Size G/6 (4mm) crochet hook *or size to obtain gauge*
■ Yarn needle

GAUGE
18 sts and 15 rows to 4"/10cm over 7-dc shell pat using size G/6 (4mm) crochet hook.
Take time to check gauge.

BLANKET
With C, ch 116.

Row 1 Work 3 dc in 4th ch from hook, [skip next 3 ch, 1 sc in each of next 7 ch, skip next 3 ch, 7 dc in next ch—shell made] 7 times, skip 3, sc in 7, skip 3, 4dc in last ch. Join A, ch 1, turn.

Row 2 With A, 1 sc in each st across, ending with 1 sc in top of t-ch. Join B, ch 1, turn.

Row 3 With B, 1 sc in each of first 4 sc, *skip 3 sc, shell in next sc, skip 3 sc, 1 sc in each of next 7 sc; rep from * across, ending last rep with skip 3 sc, 1 sc in each of last 4 sc. Join C, ch 3 (counts as 1 dc), turn.

Row 4 With C, 3 dc in first st, *skip next 3 sts, 1 sc in each of next 7 sts, skip next 3 sts, shell in next st; rep from * across, ending last rep with 4 dc in last st. Join A, ch 1, turn.

Rep rows 2–4 in stripe shell pat until piece meas approx 31" from beg.

FINISHING
Weave and trim ends.

SHELL BORDER
Rnd 1 With C, sc evenly around edge working 3 sc in each corner. Join with sl st to first sc.
Rnd 2 Ch 1, 1 sc in first sc, *skip 1 sc, 5 dc in next sc—shell made, skip 1 sc, 1 sc in next sc; rep from * around working 5-dc shell in each corner, ending last rep with omit 1 sc in next sc. Join with sl st to first sc. Fasten off.
Weave and trim ends.

Nautical and nice

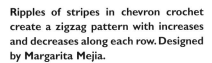

Ripples of stripes in chevron crochet create a zigzag pattern with increases and decreases along each row. Designed by Margarita Mejia.

FINISHED MEASUREMENTS
▨ 25"/63.5cm wide x 27½"/70cm long

MATERIALS
▨ 2 2.5oz/70g skeins (each approx 168yds/154m) of Lion Brand Yarn *Microspun* (micro-fiber acrylic) each in #148 turquoise (A), #109 royal blue (B), #144 lilac (C) and #194 lime (D) ③
▨ Size E/4 (3.5mm) crochet hook *or size to obtain gauge*
▨ Yarn needle

GAUGE
34 sts and 16 rows to 5"/12.5cm over pat using size E/4 (3.5mm) crochet hook.
Take time to check gauge.

Note

Join new color by working in old color to last 2 lps; leaving 6"/15cm tail, complete st by drawing new color through 2 lps and continue with new color.

BLANKET

With A, ch 171.

Row 1 (WS) Work 1 dc in 4th ch from hook, 1 dc in each of next 6 ch, *3 dc in next ch, 1 dc in each of next 7 ch, skip 2 ch, 1 dc in each of next 7 ch; rep from * across end with 3 dc in next ch, 1 dc in each of last 7 ch. Ch 3, turn. Cont to work through BL only.

Row 2 Skip first st, *1 dc in each of next 7 sts, 3 dc in next st, 1 dc in each of next 7 sts, skip 2 sts; rep from *, ending with 1 dc in each of next 7 sts, 3 dc in next st, 1 dc in each of next 6 sts, skip next st, 1 dc in last st. Join B, ch 1, turn.

Rows 3–6 With B, skip first st, *1 sc in each of next 7 sts, 3 sc in next st, 1 sc in each of next 7 sts, skip 2 sts; rep from *, ending with 1 sc in each of next 7 sts, 3 sc in next st, 1 sc in each of next 6 sts, skip next st, 1 sc in last st. Ch 1, turn. After row 6 is completed, join C, ch 3, turn.

Rows 7 and 8 With C, rep row 2. After row 8 is completed, join D, ch 1, turn.

Rows 9–12 With D, rep row 3. After row 12 is completed, join A, ch 3, turn.

Rows 13 and 14 With A, rep row 2. After row 14 is completed, join B, ch 1, turn.

Rep rows 3–14 for stripe pat st until piece measures approx 27½"/70cm from beg, ending with row 14. Fasten off.

FINISHING

Block lightly.

Crazy crayons

■■■■ ■■ □ ▭

Waves of rippling colored stripes burst with joy in this crossed stitch design by Kathleen Stuart.

FINISHED MEASUREMENTS
■ Approx 33½"/85cm square

MATERIALS
■ 4 4.4oz/125g skeins (each approx 250yds/230m) of S.R. Kertzer, Ltd. *Super 10* (mercerized cotton) in #3533 daffodil (MC) **4**
■ 1 skein each in #3764 kelly green (A), #3871 cobalt (B) and #3997 frankly scarlet (C)
■ Size G/6 (4mm) crochet hook *or size to obtain gauge*
■ Yarn needle

GAUGE
19 sts and 8 rows to 4"/10cm over ripple pat using size G/6 (4mm) crochet hook. *Take time to check gauge.*

Note Join new color at end of row by working old color to last 2 lps; leaving 6"/15cm tail, complete st by drawing new color through 2 lps and continue with new color.

STITCH GLOSSARY
Treble Crochet (tr) Yo twice and draw lp, [yo and through 2 lps] 3 times.
Dc2tog (over 2 sts) [Yo and draw lp in next st, yo and through 2 lps] twice, yo and through all 3 lps.

Back Crossed Treble Crochet (BCtr) Skip specified sts, 1 tr in next st, ch 1, working behind last tr made, 1 tr in specified st.

Stripe Pattern *2 rows MC, 1 row A, 2 rows MC, 1 row B, 2 rows MC, 1 row C; rep from * (9 rows) for stripe pat.

BLANKET
With MC, ch 163.
Row 1 1 Dc in 4th ch from hook, *(skip 2 chs, 1 tr in next st, ch 1, working behind last tr made, 1 tr in first skipped ch—BCtr made, ch 1, skip 3 chs, tr in next st, ch 1, working behind last tr made, 1 tr in second skipped ch)**, [dc2tog] twice; rep between ( ) once, then 2 dc in each of next 2 chs; rep from * across, ending last rep at **, 2 dc in last ch. Turn.
Row 2 Ch 3 (counts as 1 dc), 1 dc in first st, *(skip 2 sts, 1 tr in next st, ch 1, working behind last tr made, 1 tr in first skipped st, ch 1, skip 3 sts, 1 tr in next st, ch 1, working behind last tr made, 1 tr in second skipped st)**, [dc2tog] twice; rep between ( ) once, then 2 dc in each of next 2 sts; rep from * across, ending last rep at **, 2 dc in last st. Join A. Turn.
Row 3 Ch 1, 2 sc in first st, *1 sc in each of next 7 sts, [sc2tog] twice, 1 sc in each of next 7 sts**, 2 sc in each of next 2 sts; rep from * across, ending last rep at **, 2 sc in last st. Join MC. Turn.

Row 4 Ch 3 (counts as 1 dc), 1 dc in first st, *(skip 2 sts, 1 tr in next st, ch 1, working behind last tr made, 1 tr in first skipped st, ch 1, skip 3 sts, 1 tr in next st, ch 1, working behind last tr made, 1 tr in second skipped st)**, [dc2tog] twice; rep between ( ) once, then 2 dc in each of next 2 sts; rep from * across, ending last rep at **, 2 dc in last st. Turn.

Row 5 Rep row 4. Join B.

Rows 6–68 Repeat rows 3–5 and cont stripe pat. Fasten off.

FINISHING
Weave in ends.

TRELLIS BLANKET

Lavender lullaby

Chain stitches make up this lovely lace pattern designed by Jennifer Appleby.

FINISHED MEASUREMENTS
■ Approx 27"/68.5cm wide x 44½"/113cm long

MATERIALS
■ 7 1.75oz/50g balls (each approx 202yds/185m) of Karabella Light-Weight *Supercashmere* (cashmere) in #82 Indigo
■ Size C/2 (2.75mm) crochet hook *or size to obtain gauge*
■ Yarn needle

GAUGE
26 sts and 23 rows to 4"/10cm in chain lace pat using size C/2 (2.75mm) crochet hook.
Take time to check gauge.

BLANKET

Ch 178.

Row 1 (WS) Work 1 sc in 2nd ch from hook, 1 sc in each ch to end—177 sc. Turn.

Row 2 Ch 1, 1 sc in each of first 3 sc, *ch 5, skip 3 sc, 1 sc in each of next 5 sc; rep from * to last 6 sc, ch 5, skip 3 sc, 1 sc in each of last 3 sc. Turn.

Row 3 Ch 1, 1 sc in each of first 2 sc, *ch 3, 1 sc in next ch-5 sp, ch 3, skip 1 sc, 1 sc in each of next 3 sc; rep from * to last rep,

skip 1 sc, 1 sc in each of last 2 sc. Turn.

Row 4 Ch 1, 1 sc in first sc, *ch 3, 1 sc in next ch-3 sp, 1 sc in next sc, 1 sc in next ch-3 sp, ch 3, skip 1 sc, 1 sc in next sc; rep from * to end. Turn.

Row 5 Ch 5 (counts as 1 dc and ch 2), 1 sc in next ch-3 sp, 1 sc in each of next 3 sc, 1 sc in next ch-3 sp, *ch 5, 1 sc in next ch-3 sp, 1 sc in next 3 sc, 1 sc in next ch-3 sp; rep from * to last sc, ch 2, 1 dc in last sc. Turn.

Row 6 Ch 1, 1 sc in first dc, ch 3, skip 1 sc, 1 sc in each of next 3 sc, *ch 3, 1 sc in next ch-5 sp, ch 3, skip 1 sc, 1 sc in each of next 3 sc; rep from * to last ch-2 sp, ch 3, 1 sc in 3rd ch of beg ch-5. Turn.

Row 7 Ch 1, 1 sc in first sc, 1 sc in next ch-3 sp, ch 3, skip 1 sc, 1 sc in next sc, *ch 3, 1 sc in next ch-3 sp, 1 sc in next sc, 1 sc in next ch-3 sp, ch 3, skip 1 sc, 1 sc in next sc; rep from * to last ch-3 sp, ch 3, 1 sc in ch-3 sp, 1 sc in last sc. Turn.

Row 8 Ch 1, 1 sc in each of first 2 sc, *1 sc in next ch-3 sp, ch 5, 1 sc in next ch-3 sp, 1 sc in each of next 3 sc; rep from * , end last rep with 1 sc in each of last 2 sc. Turn.

Rep rows 3–8 until piece meas approx 42½" from beg. DO NOT FASTEN OFF.

TOP EDGING

Next Row (WS) Ch 1, 1 sc in each sc and 3 sc in each ch-5 sp—177 sc. Turn.

Row 1 (RS) Ch 1, 1 sc in each sc across. Turn.

Row 2 Ch 1, 1 sc in each of first 3 sc, *ch 9, skip 3 sc, 1 sc in each of next 5 sc; rep from * to last 6 sc, ch 9, skip 3 sc, 1 sc in each of last 3 sc. Turn.

Row 3 Ch 1, 1 sc in each of first 2 sc, *ch 5, 1 sc in next ch-9 sp, ch 5, skip 1 sc, 1 sc in each of next 3 sc; rep from * , ending last rep with 1 sc in each of last 2 sc. Turn.

Row 4 Ch 1, 1 sc in first sc, *ch 5, skip 1 sc, 1 sc in next sc; rep from * to end. Turn.

Row 5 Ch 1, 1 sc in first sc, *ch 5, [sl st, (ch 7, sl st) 3 times] in next sc, ch 5, 1 sc in next sc; rep from * to end. Fasten off.

BOTTOM EDGING

Attach yarn to right edge.

Row 1 (RS) Ch 1, 1 sc in each foundation ch lp across—177 sc. Turn.

Rows 2–5 Rep rows 2–5 of Top Edging.

FINISHING

Block to finished measurements. Weave in ends.

FLORAL BLANKET

Salt water taffy

Candi Jensen's floral embellishments complement this striped pattern. A lovely scalloped edging completes the picture.

FINISHED MEASUREMENTS
■ Approx 32"/81.5cm square

MATERIALS
■ 3 5oz/140g skeins (each approx 256yds/234m) of Red Heart/Coats & Clark *Soft Yarn* (acrylic) in #4601 off white (MC) (**4**)
■ 1 skein each in #4614 black (A), #6768 pink (B)
■ Yarn needle

GAUGE
11 sts and 10 rows to 4"/10cm over hdc/sc stripe pat using size I/9 (5.50mm) crochet hook. *Take time to check gauge.*

STITCH GLOSSARY
Treble Crochet (tr) Yo twice and draw lp, [yo and through 2 lps] 3 times.

BLANKET
With MC, ch 83.

Row 1 Work 1 hdc in 3rd ch from hook and in each ch across. Turn.

Rows 2–4 With MC, ch 2 (counts as 1 hdc), 1 hdc in each hdc across. Join A at end of row 4, turn.

Rows 5 and 6 With A, ch 1, 1 sc in first and in each st across. Join MC at end of row 6, turn.

Row 7 With MC, ch 2 (counts as 1 hdc), 1 hdc in each st across. Turn.

Rep rows 2–7 for stripe pat 10 times more, then rep rows 2–4 once. Fasten off.

EDGING
Row 1 With B, ch 1 and sc evenly around edges, working 3 sc in each corner. Join with sl st to first sc. Turn.

Row 2 Ch 3 (counts as 1 hdc and ch 1), skip 1 st, *1 hdc in next st, ch 1, skip 1 st; rep from * to corner, (1 hdc, ch 1, 1 hdc) in corner; rep from * around. Join with sl st to 2nd ch of beg ch-3. Turn.

Row 3 Ch 1, sc in same sp as joining, *3 dc in next hdc, sc in next hdc; rep from * around, joining with sl st to 1st sc.

Row 4 Ch 1, 1 sc in same sp as joining, *skip 2 sts, 2 dc in next st, 3 tr in next st, 2 dc in next st, skip 2 sts, 1 sc in next st; rep from * around with 3 tr in each corner. Join and fasten off.

Large Flower
(make 1)
With MC, ch 5 and join with a sl st to form ring.

Rnd 1 Ch 1, 14 sc over ring. Join with sl st to beg ch-1.

Rnd 2 [Ch 4, skip 2 sts, sl st in next st] 4 times, end with ch 4, skip last 2 sts. Join with sl st in first ch of beg ch-4—5 ch-4 loops.

Rnd 3 Ch 1 (counts as sc), (1 dc, 2 tr, 1 dc,

1 sc) in first ch-4 sp, * (1 sc, 1 dc, 2 tr, 1 dc, 1 sc) in next ch-4 sp; rep from * around 3 times. Join sl st to beg ch-1.

Rnd 4 [Ch 5, sl st between next 2 sc between petals] 4 times, end ch 5, sl st in first ch of beg ch-5—5 ch-5 lps. Fasten off.

Rnd 5 Join B to any ch-5 lp and ch 1, *(1 sc, 2 dc, 2 tr, 2 dc, 1 sc) in next ch-5 lp; rep from * around 4 times. Join with sl st to beg ch-1. Fasten off.

SMALL FLOWER

Make 2 flowers with MC for rnd 1 and with B for rnds 2 and 3.

Make 1 flower with MC and 1 flower with B for rnds 1–3.

Ch 5 and join with sl st to form ring.

Rnd 1 Ch 1, 14 sc over ring. Join with sl st to beg ch-1.

Rnd 2 [Ch 4, skip 2 sts, sl st in next st] 4 times, end ch 4, skip 2 sts, sl st in first ch of beg ch-4—5 ch-4 lps.

Rnd 3 Ch 1 (counts as 1 sc), (1 dc, 2 tr, 1 dc 1 sc) in first ch-4 sp, * (1 sc, 1 dc, 2 tr, 1 dc, 1 sc) in next ch 4 sp; rep from * around 3 times. Join sl st to beg ch-1. Fasten off.

BOBBLE CENTER

(make 5)

With A, ch 2.

Row 1 In 2nd ch from hook, [yo and draw lp, yo and draw through 2 lps] 4 times, yo and through all 5 loops on hook. Fasten off, leaving tail for sewing.

FINISHING

Weave in ends. Sew bobble center to flowers. Sew flowers onto blanket.

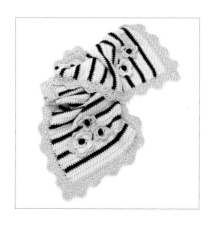

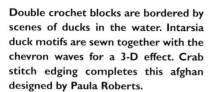

Double crochet blocks are bordered by scenes of ducks in the water. Intarsia duck motifs are sewn together with the chevron waves for a 3-D effect. Crab stitch edging completes this afghan designed by Paula Roberts.

■ 33"/84cm wide x 41½"/106cm long
■ Each dc block approx 8"/20.5cm wide x 8"/20.5cm.

MATERIALS
■ 8 1.75oz/50g balls (each approx 121yds/111m) of GGH/Muench *Maxima* (Superwash merino wool) in #1 ecru (MC) ⑤
■ 7 balls in #42 blue (A)
■ 5 balls in #3 yellow (B)
■ 1 ball in #4 orange (C)
■ Size E/4 (3.5mm) crochet hook *or size to obtain gauge*
■ 1 skein embroidery floss in black
■ Yarn needle

GAUGE
18 sts and 9½ rows to 4"/10cm over dc using size E/4 (3.5mm) crochet hook.
Take time to check gauge.

Notes
1 Intarsia color blocks are worked with separate balls of yarn or bobbins. The yarns are not carried across or worked over by new colors.

2 Join new color by working st in old color to last 2 lps; leaving 6"/15cm tail, complete st by drawing new color through 2 lps and continue with new color.

STITCH GLOSSARY
BL Work through back loop only.
Dc2tog (over 2 sts) [Yo and draw lp in next st, yo and draw through 2 lps] twice, yo and draw through all 3 lps.

SOLID SQUARES
(make 6 blue and 6 ecru)
Ch 38.
Row 1 Work 1 dc in 4th ch from hook (ch 3 counts as 1 dc), 1 dc in each ch across—36 dc. Turn.
Row 2 Ch 3 (counts as 1 dc), skip first dc, 1 dc in each dc across, end with dc in top of ch-3. Turn.
Rep row 2 until square measures approx 8"/20.5cm. Fasten off.

DUCK SQUARE
(make 8)
Duck
With MC, ch 37. Work duck chart 1 as foll:
Row 1 (RS) Work 1 sc in 2nd ch from the hook and in next 9 ch; with B, 1 sc in next 18 ch; with MC, 1 sc in last 8 ch. Turn.
Rows 2–30 Ch 1, sc in each sc and foll chart II for duck motif. Fasten off.

Water

With A, ch 39.

Row 1 Inserting hook under "V" of lps, 1 dc in 4th ch, *1 dc in each of next 3 ch, [dc2tog over next 2 ch] twice, 1 dc in each of next 3 ch, [2 dc in next ch] twice; rep from *, ending last rep with [2 dc in next ch] once. The back lps form the waves of the water. Turn.

Row 2 Ch 3 (counts as 1 dc) and work in BL only, 1 dc in first st, *1 dc in each of next 3 sts, [dc2tog over next 2 sts] twice, 1 dc in each of next 3 sts, [2 dc in next st] twice; rep from *, ending last rep with 2 dc in last st. Turn.

Rows 3–5 Rep row 2.

Row 6 Ch 1, 1 sc in each st across. Turn.

Row 7 Ch 1, 1 sc in each st across. Fasten off. This edge is the bottom of the duck square.

Wing

With B, ch 3. Join with sl st to form ring.

Rnd 1 Ch 2, 7 hdc in ring. Join with sl st to top of beg ch-2.

Rnd 2 Ch 3, 2 hdc in joining sp, sl st in next st. Fasten off.

Assembling Duck Squares

With wave edge upwards, position against bottom edge of duck motif so that length of block measures approx 8"/20.5cm. Sew water to front of duck in backstitch, then hem edge to back of water. Embroider face on each duck. Tack wing to side of duck.

Edgings

With B, sc evenly around each solid and duck square, with 3 sc in each corner. Fasten off.

Arrange squares according to Chart II and sew together.

Rnd 1 With B, sc evenly around entire blanket, with 3 sc in each corner. Join with sl st to first sc.

Rnd 2 With B, ch 1, *working from left to right, 1 sc in next st to right, ch 1, skip 1; rep from * around. Join with sl st to first sc. Fasten off.

Weave in all ends and block.

Chart 1

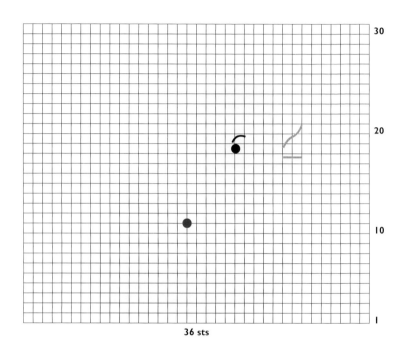

30

20

10

1

36 sts

Color Key

☐ Ecru (MC)

☐ Yellow (B)

Stitch Key

● Attach Wing

— Straight Stitch

● Eye

— Straight Stitch

Chart II

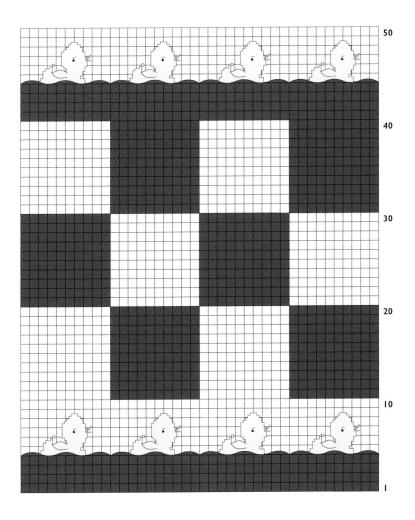

50

40

30

20

10

1

AMISH-STYLE BLANKET

Star quality

"Nine-Patches" of stars in intarsia crochet and "Flying Geese" triangles in jacquard crochet border come to life in this blanket designed by **Ann E. Smith.**

FINISHED MEASUREMENTS
▨ 32½"/82.5cm wide x 34"/86.5cm long

MATERIALS
▨ 6 1.75oz/50g balls (each approx 104yds/95m) of Rowan/Westminster Fibers, Inc. *Luxury Cotton DK* (cotton/viscose/silk) in #259 black (MC) ③
▨ 4 balls in #256 broncho (A)
▨ 2 balls in #255 pagoda (B)
▨ 1 ball each in #250 marble (C), #252 tang (D), #254 slipper (E), #253 crisp (F)
▨ Size F/5 (3.75mm) crochet hook *or size to obtain gauge*
▨ Yarn needle

GAUGE
16 sts and 16 rows to 4"/10cm in sc using size F/5 (3.75mm) crochet hook.
Take time to check gauge.

Notes
I Star blocks in intarsia crochet are worked with separate balls of yarn or bobbins. The yarns are not carried across or worked over by new color.
2 Triangle border in jacquard crochet is worked with unused yarn carried across top of row and worked over with new color.

3 Join new color by working st in old color to last 2 lps; leaving 6"/15cm tail, complete st by drawing new color through 2 lps and continue with new color.

COLOR BLOCKS
(make 9)
All blocks are made with color MC as background and specified color for star design.
Make 2 each with color C, color E, color F.
Make 1 each with color A, color B, color D.
With MC, ch 37.
Row I (RS) Work 1 sc in 2nd ch from hook and in each ch across—36 sc. Turn.
Rows 2–37 Continue with rows 2–37 of chart I in sc.
Row 38 (WS) With MC, ch 1, 1 sc in each sc across. Fasten off.

BORDERS
Arrange blocks in order of chart layout and whipstitch together.
Top and Bottom
(make 1 each)
With A, ch 12 and work from chart II.
Row I (WS) 1 Sc in 2nd ch from hook and in each ch across—11 sts. Turn.
Rows 2–5 Work with A for background and with B for triangle motif. Rep last 4 rows 26 times more. Turn.
Last Row Ch 1, 1 sc in each sc across. Fasten off.
Whipstitch borders to top and bottom edges.

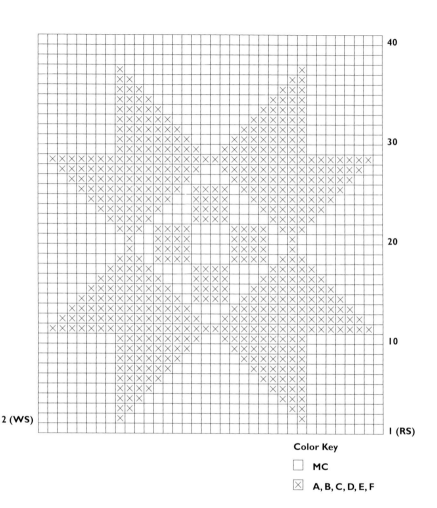

40

30

20

10

2 (WS)

1 (RS)

Color Key

☐ MC

☒ A, B, C, D, E, F

R5 (WS)

R1 (WS)

R2 (RS)

Color Key

☐ A

☒ B

Side

(make 2)

Work same as top and bottom border, but rep rows 2–5 for 28 times.

Whipstitch to right and left side edges.

Corner Block

With the RS facing, join A with sl st in first sc at right edge of bottom border.

Row 1 Ch 1, sc in same sc and next 10 sc, sl st in first and second sts of side border. Turn.

Row 2 Ch 1, skip 2 sl sts, 1 sc in each 11 sc. Turn.

Row 3 Ch 1, 1 sc in each 11 sc, sl st in next 2 sts of side border. Turn.

Row 4 Ch 1, skip 2 sl sts, 1 sc in each 11 sc. Turn.

Rows 5–10 Rep rows 3 and 4. Turn.

Row 11 Ch 1, 1 sc in 11 sc, sl st in last st of side border. Fasten off.

Rep for rem 3 corners.

FINISHING

Weave in ends.

With A and RS facing, sl st around edges.

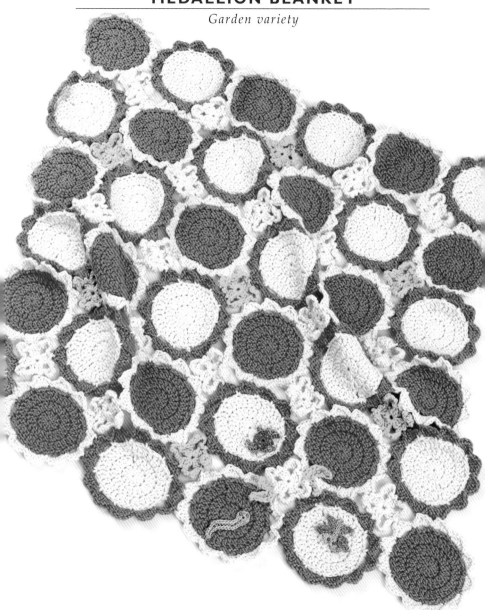

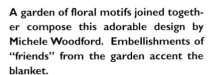

A garden of floral motifs joined together compose this adorable design by Michele Woodford. Embellishments of "friends" from the garden accent the blanket.

FINISHED MEASUREMENTS
■ 30"/76.2cm square

MATERIALS
■ 3 3.5oz/100g skeins (each approx 171yds/156m) of Bernat *Cotton Tots* (cotton) each in #90421 strawberry (MC) and #90615 sunshine (CC) ■
■ 1 skein in #90712 lime berry (LF)
■ 1 skein (each approx 16.4 yds/15m) of DMC Perle Cotton #3 (cotton) each in #210 medium lavender (E1), #351 coral (E2), #605 very light cranberry (E3), #954 nile green (E4) and #3348 light yellow green (E5)
■ Size C/2 (2.75mm) and H/8 (5mm) crochet hooks *or sizes to obtain gauge*
■ Yarn needle
■ Embroidery needle

GAUGE
1 dc circle motif without petal edging measures 3½" in diameter, using size H/8 (5mm) crochet hook. *Take time to check gauge.*

Notes
1 Follow diagram for motif, color and appliqué placements.

2 Motif joining starts from right to left and from top to bottom.

QUILT
Circle Motif
Note All circle motifs are made first, then petal edging is added afterward with joining. (make 18 each of MC and CC)
Make adjustable sl lp.
Rnd 1 Ch 3 (counts as 1 dc), 11 dc around lp, pull lp to close rn—12 dc. Join with sl st to top of beg ch-3.
Rnd 2 Ch 3 (counts as 1 dc), 1 dc in first st, 2 dc in each st around—24 dc. Join with sl st to top of beg ch-3.
Rnd 3 Ch 3 (counts as 1 dc), *2 dc in next st, 1 dc in next st; rep from * around ending last rep with 2 dc in next st—36 dc. Join with sl st to top of beg ch-3.
Rnd 4 Ch 1, *1 sc in next st, ch 3, skip 2 sts; rep from * around—12 petal chs. Join with sl st to first sc. Fasten off.

Adding Petals and Joining Motifs
Note On MC motifs, use CC for petals; on CC motifs, use MC for petals.
Motif 1 *Sl st in sc on petal ch row, (1 sc, 1 hdc, 2 dc, 1 hdc, 1 sc) in ch sp; rep from * around—12 petals. Join with sl st to first sl st. Fasten off.
Motifs 2–7, 13, 19, 25, 31 *Sl st in sc, (1 sc, 1 hdc, 2 dc, 1 hdc, 1 sc) in ch sp— full petal; rep from * around until 2 ch sps rem, [sl st in sc, (1 sc, 1 hdc, 1 dc) in next

ch sp, join with 1 sc in between 2 dc of motif 1, (1 dc, 1 hdc, 1 sc) in same ch sp of motif 2] twice—joining petals. Join with sl st to first sl st. Fasten off.

Motifs 8–12, 14–18, 20–24, 26–30, 32–36

Work petal row and joining as above, rep full petal in non-joining ch sps, and rep between [ ] twice for joining petals to right and previous row motifs.

Small Flower Motifs

Note Flower motifs are worked and joined in rnd 2 with adjacent 2 petals of motifs.

Ch 3 and join with sl st to form ring.

Rnd 1 Ch 3 (counts as 1 dc), 2 dc in ring, [ch 3, 3 dc in ring] 3 times, ch 3. Join with sl st to beg ch-3.

Rnd 2 (joining) *Sl st in next st of flower, sl st between 2 dc of petal 1–joining, sl st in next dc and ch sp of flower, ch 3, ([yo and draw lp, yo and draw through 2 lps] twice in same ch sp, yo and through all 3 lps)—Dc2CL, ch 3; rep from * around joining to petals 2, 3 and 4. Join with sl st to beg sl st.

Small Flower Motif Leaf Accents

*With larger hook and LF, draw lp in sl st above 3-dc group. Ch 8, sl st into same st, 1 sc in next st, ch 8, sl st to same st; rep from * around to opposite side of small flower motif. Fasten off and sew to quilt.

(make 1 of each, or more if desired)

Note Lp(s) is the back lp on foundation ch.

Wiggly Worm

With smaller hook and E5, ch 17.

Rnd (1st half) 1 Sc in 3rd lp from hook, 1 sc in each of next 3 lps, skip 1 lp, 1 sc in each of next 4 lps, 2 sc in next lp, 1 sc in each of next 4 lps, 8 hdc in last lp.

Rnd (2nd half) Working on opposite side of foundation ch, 1 sc in each of next 3 lps, skip 1 lp, 1 sc in each of next 4 lps, 2 sc in next lp, 1 sc in each of next 3 lps, sl st in each of last 2 lps. Fasten off leaving long tail for sewing.

With embroidery needle weave in tail from beg through lps of "head" to close. With E3, make 2 french knots for eyes.

Butterfly

Antennae

(make 2)

With E5, ch 4 and join with sl st to first ch. Ch 12 and sl st in 4th ch from hook. Fasten off and carefully weave end to WS.

Body

With E4, ch 10 and sl st in 3rd lp from hook, sl st in next 6 lps, (sl st, 6 sc) in last lp, sl st in 7 lps around opposite side of foundation ch. Fasten off and weave end to WS.

Bottom Wing

With E3, draw ch from behind "body" and

through 4th lp from bottom. Ch 7 and sl st in 3rd lp from hook, skip 1 lp, 1 sc in next lp, 2 hdc in next 2 lps, sl st into last st worked, then sl st in next 'body' lp.

Top Wing

With E3, ch 10 and sl st in 3rd lp from hook, skip 1 lp, 1 dc in next lp, 1 tr in each of next 2 lps, 1 dc in next lp, 1 sc in last lp. Secure top wing to body with 1 sl st. Use hook to draw thread to WS of body then pull 1 lp through to RS opposite of bottom wing. Work bottom and top wing to correspond to other side.

With E2, make 2 french knots for eyes and

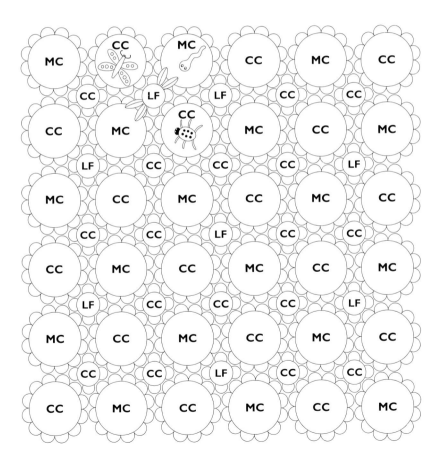

with E1, 3 french knots on each wing.

Spider

Body

With E2, ch 3 and join with sl st to form ring.

Rnd I Ch 3, 14 dc in ring. Join with sl st to top of beg ch-3.

Rnd 2 (head) Ch 1, 3 hdc in next st (top 2 lps), join head to body with sl st. Fasten off and weave end to WS. With embroidery needle use tail to tighten center hole in body.

Rnd 3 (legs) With E1, *draw lp from WS to RS on 2nd lp below "head." Ch 5, sl st in 3rd ch from hook, sl st in each of next 3 lps. Take hook out of last sl st, and from WS draw last sl st to back and make 1 sl st; rep from * in next 3 lps of body—4 legs. Rep rnd 3 for other side.

With E4, make 2 french knots for eyes. With E1, make 6 french knots (spots) on spider's body.

FINISHING

Weave in ends to like colors. Sew appliqués to quilt using diagram for placement. Block lightly if desired.

Hydrangea bouquet

Get some "relief" and crochet this textured design by Marty Miller. Front and back post double crochet stitches create a diagonal pattern throughout the blanket.

FINISHED MEASUREMENTS
- 28½"/72.5cm wide x 33"/84cm long

MATERIALS
- 4 1.75oz/50g skeins (each approx 88yds/80m) of Nashua Handknits/ Westminster Fibers, Inc. *Wooly Stripes* (wool) in #6 lilac blossoms 🔲
- Size I/9 (5.5mm) crochet hook *or size to obtain gauge*
- Yarn needle

GAUGE
13 sts to 4"/10cm over dc using I/9 crochet hook. *Take time to check gauge.*

STITCH GLOSSARY
Foundation Double Crochet (Fdc) Yo and draw lp, yo and draw through 1 lp – chain made, [yo and draw through 2 loops] twice.

Front Post Double Crochet (FPdc) Yo and insert hook from front to back to front around post (vertical bar) of indicated st, [yo and draw through 2 lps] twice.

Back Post Double Crochet (BPdc) Yo and insert hook from back to front to back around post (vertical bar) of indicated st, [yo and draw through 2 lps] twice.

BLANKET
Ch 4.

Foundation Row 1 (WS) 1 Fdc in 4th ch from hook, *1 Fdc in ch at base of previous Fdc; rep from * until there are 82 Fdc counting ch 3 of beg ch-4. Turn.

Row 2 (RS) Ch 2, skip first st, *FPdc around each of next 4 sts, BPdc around each of next 4 sts; rep from * 9 times, end with 1 hdc between last 2 sts. Turn.

Row 3 Ch 2, skip first st, FPdc around each of next 3 sts, *BPdc around each of next 4 sts, FPdc around each of next 4 sts, rep from * 8 times, end last rep with FPdc around next st, 1 hdc between last 2 sts. Turn.

Row 4 Ch 2, skip first st, BPdc around each of next 2 sts, *FPdc around each of next 4 sts, BPdc around each of next 4 sts; rep from * 8 times, end last rep with BPdc around each of next 2 sts, 1 hdc between last 2 sts. Turn.

Row 5 Ch 2, skip first st, FPdc around

next st, *BPdc around each of next 4 sts, FPdc around each of next 4 sts; rep from * 8 times, end last rep with FPdc around each of next 3 sts, 1 hdc between last 2 sts. Turn.

Row 6 Ch 2, skip first st, *BPdc around each of next 4 sts, FPdc around each of next 4 sts; rep from * 9 times, end last rep with 1 hdc between last 2 sts. Turn.

Row 7 Ch 2, skip first st, BPdc around each of next 3 sts, *FPdc around each of next 4 sts, BPdc around each of next 4 sts; rep from * 8 times, end last rep with BPdc around next st, 1 hdc between last 2 sts. Turn.

Row 8 Ch 2, skip first st, FPdc around each of next 2 sts, *BPdc around next 4 sts, FPdc around next 4 sts; rep from * 8 times, end last rep with FPdc around next 2 sts, 1 hdc between last 2 sts. Turn.

Row 9 Ch 2, skip first st, BPdc around next st, *FPdc around each of next 4 sts, BPdc around each of next 4 sts; rep from * 8 times, end last rep with BPdc around each of next 3 sts, 1 hdc between last 2 sts. Turn.

Rows 10–73 Rep rows 2–9 eight times.

Row 74 Rep row 2. DO NOT FASTEN OFF.

EDGING

Notes

1 Mark corner sts, and move markers up for each round.

2 The ch-3 at the beg of rnd 3, and the ch-2 at the beg of rnds 4 and 5, count as the first sts for the next rounds.

Rnd 1 Ch 1, 2 sc in corner st, (mark first sc for corner), 1 sc in each st along side edge to corner, 3 sc in corner st, (mark 2nd sc for this and next 2 corners), 1 sc in each st at bottom of starting edge, 3 sc in corner st, 1 sc in each st along side edge, 3 sc in corner st, 1 sc in each st along top edge, end 1 sc in same corner as first 2 sc. Join with sl st to first sc. Do not turn.

Rnd 2 Ch 1, 1 sc in each sc and 3 sc in each corner sc around. Join with sl st to first sc.

Rnd 3 Ch 3, skip the first st, 1 dc in each sc and 3 dc in each corner sc around. Join with sl st to top of ch-3.

Rnd 4 Ch 2, skip the first st, BPdc in each dc and 3 BPdc in each corner dc around. Join with sl st to top of ch-2.

Rnds 5 and 6 Repeat Rnd 4. Fasten off.

LACE BLANKET

Pistachio parfait

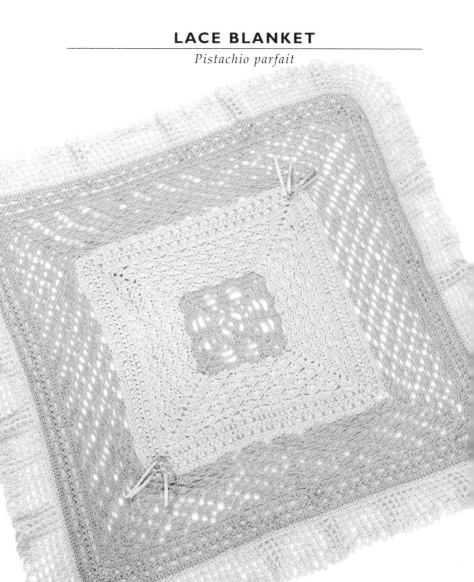

■■■◻

In this design by Susan Shildmyer, bands of fans, Vs, eyelets and shells are worked in the round from a center motif. Ribbons are woven in eyelet bands. The blanket is finished with a filet stitch ruffle edging.

FINISHED MEASUREMENTS
- 34"/86.4cm square

MATERIALS
- 4 1.75oz/50g hanks (each approx 146yds/133m) of Blue Sky Alpacas *Alpaca Silk* (alpaca/silk) each in #136 champagne (MC) and in #116 spring (CC) (4)
- Size G/6 (4mm) and H/8 (5mm) crochet hooks *or sizes to obtain gauge*
- 10yds ½"/6mm ribbon in MC
- 5yds ½"/6mm ribbon in CC
- Yarn needle

GAUGE
18 sts and 11 rows to 4"/10cm in dc using size H/8 (5mm) crochet hook.
Take time to check gauge.

STITCH GLOSSARY
Corner (2 Dc, ch 3, 2 dc) in ch sp.
Fan (3 Dc, ch 1, 3 dc) in ch-1 sp of V-St.
V-St (1 Hdc, ch 1, 1 hdc) in same st.
Back Crossed DC (BCdc) (over 2 sps) Skip ch sp, 1 dc in next ch sp, working behind last dc made, 1 dc in skipped ch sp.
Shell (5 Dc) in same st.

BLANKET
Center Motif
With MC, ch 8. Join with sl st to first ch to form ring.

Rnd 1 Ch 1, 16 sc in ring. Join with sl st to first sc—16 sc.

Rnd 2 Ch 1, 1 sc in same sp, *ch 7, skip 3 sts, 1 sc; rep from *, ending last rep with skip 3 sts—4 ch-7 sp. Join with sl st to first sc.

Rnd 3 Sl st across to 3rd ch of first ch sp, ch 3 (counts as 1 dc), 1 dc in same ch, *ch 2, 2 dc, ch 3 in first ch sp, dc2tog (inserting hook into first ch-7 sp for 1st leg and into second ch-7 sp for 2nd leg), ch 3, 2 dc in second ch-7 sp; rep from * around, ending last rep with dc2tog, ch 3. Join with sl st to top of beg ch-3.

Rnd 4 Sl st in next dc and next ch, ch 3 (counts as 1 dc), 1 dc in same ch, *ch 3, 2 dc in ch-3 sp, ch 3, skip 2 dc, 3 dc in next ch-3 sp, 1 dc in top of dc2tog, 3 dc in next ch-3 sp, ch 3, skip 2 sts, 2 dc in next ch sp; rep from *, ending last rep with ch 3, skip 2 sts. Join with sl st to top of beg ch-3.

Rnd 5 Sl st in next dc and next ch, ch 3, 2 dc in ch, *ch 3, 3 dc in first ch sp, ch 6, skip (2 dc, ch 3, 2 dc), 1 dc in each of next 5 dc, ch 6, skip (1 dc, ch 3, 2 dc), 3 dc in next ch-3 sp; rep from *, ending last rep with ch 6, skip (1 dc, ch 3, 2 dc). Join with sl st to top of beg ch-3.

Rnd 6 Ch 3 (counts as 1 dc), 1 dc in each of next 2 dc, *(3 dc, ch 5, 3 dc) in first ch sp, 1 dc in each of next 3 dc, ch 6, skip ch-6 sp and 1 dc, 1 dc in each of next 3 dc, ch 6, skip 1 dc and ch-6 sp, 1 dc in each of next 3 dc; rep from *, ending last rep skip 1 dc and ch-6 sp. Join with sl st to top of beg ch-3.

Rnd 7 Ch 3 (counts as 1 dc), skip 1 dc, 1 dc in each of the next 5 dc, *work Corner, 1 dc in each of next 6 dc, 6 dc in ch-6 sp, 1 dc in each of next 3 dc, 6 dc in ch-6 sp, 1 dc in each of next 6 dc; rep from *, ending last rep with 6 dc in ch-6 sp. Join with sl st to top of beg ch-3—136 sts. Fasten off.

Fan Stitch Band

Rnd 8 Join CC to next dc and ch 3 (count as 1 dc), (2 dc, ch 1, 3 dc) in same st, *skip 3 dc, 1 sc in each of next 2 dc, Corner in ch sp, 1 sc in each of next 2 dc, skip 3, [(3 dc, ch 1, 3 dc) in next st, skip 3 dc, 1 sc, ch 1, skip 1, 1 sc, skip 3] twice, (3 dc, ch 1, 3 dc) in next st; rep from *, ending last rep with [(3 dc, ch 1, 3 dc) in next st, skip 3 dc, 1 sc, ch 1, skip 1, 1 sc, skip 3] twice. Join with sl st to top of beg ch-3.

Rnd 9 Ch 3, skip 3 dc, *1 sc in ch sp of Fan, ch 3, skip 3 dc and 1 sc, V-St in next sc, 1 dc in each of next 2 sts, Corner in ch sp, 1 dc in each of next 2 dc, V-St in next st, [ch 3, skip 1 sc and 3 dc, 1 sc in ch sp of Fan, ch 3, skip 3 dc and 1 sc, V-St in ch sp] twice, ch 3; rep from *, ending last rep with skip 1. Join with sl st to base of beg ch-3.

Rnd 10 Ch 3, 1 sc in 3 ch sp, ch 1, skip 1 sc, 1 sc in ch-3 sp, *Fan in next ch-1 sp, skip 3, 1 sc in each of next 2 dc, Corner in ch sp, 1 sc in each of next 2 sts, skip 3, [Fan in ch-1 sp, 1 sc in next ch-3 sp, skip 1 sc, ch 1, 1 sc next ch-3 sp] 3 times; rep from *, ending last rep with (3 dc, ch 1, 2 dc) in ch-1 sp. Join with sl st to top of beg ch-3.

Rnd 11 2 Sl st, ch 3 (counts as 1 hdc and ch 1), 1 hdc in sl st, ch 3, skip 3 dc, 1 sc in ch sp of Fan, *ch 3, skip 3 dc and 1 sc, V-St in next sc, 1 dc in each of next 2 sts, Corner in ch sp, 1 dc in each of next 2 sts, V-St in next st, [ch 3, skip 1 sc and 3 dc, 1 sc in ch sp of Fan, ch 3, skip 3 dc and 1 sc, V-St in ch sp] twice, ch 3, skip 1 sc and 3 dc, 1 sc in ch sp of Fan; rep from *, ending last rep with ch 3. Join with sl st in 2nd ch of beg ch-3.

Rnd 12 Ch 3, (2 dc, ch 1, 3 dc) in ch-1 sp, 1 sc in ch-3 sp, skip 1 sc, 1 sc in ch-3 sp, Fan in ch-1 sp, *skip 3, 1 sc in each of next 2 sts, Corner in ch sp, 1 sc in each of next 2 sts, skip 3, [Fan, 1 sc in ch-3 sp, skip 1, ch 1, 1 sc in ch-3 sp] 4 times, Fan in next ch-1 sp; rep from *, ending last rep with [Fan, 1 sc in ch-3 sp, skip 1, ch 1, 1 sc in ch-3 sp] 3 times. Join with sl st to top of beg ch-3.

Rnd 13 Ch 3, 1 sc in ch sp of Fan, ch 3, V-St in ch-1 sp, ch 3, 1 sc in ch sp of Fan, *ch 3, skip 3 dc and 1 sc, V-St in next sc,

1 dc in each of next 2 sts, Corner in ch sp, 1 dc in each of next 2 sts, V-St in next st, ch 3, 1 sc in ch sp of Fan, [ch 3, V-St in ch-1 sp, ch 3, 1 sc in ch sp of Fan] 4 times; rep from *, ending last rep with [ch 3, V-St in ch-1 sp, ch 3, 1 sc in ch sp of Fan] twice, ch 3, V-St in ch-1 sp. Join with sl st to base of beg ch-3.

Rnd 14 Ch 3, [1 sc in ch-3 sp, skip 1 sc, 1 sc in ch-3 sp, Fan in ch sp] twice, *skip 3, 1 sc in each of next 2 dc, Corner in ch sp, 2 sc, skip 3, [Fan in ch-1 sp, 1 sc in next ch-3 sp, skip 1 sc, ch 1, 1 sc in next ch-3 sp] 5 times, Fan in ch-1 sp; rep from *, ending last rep with [Fan, 1 sc in ch-3 sp, skip 1, ch 1, 1 sc in ch-3 sp] 3 times. Join with sl st to top of beg ch-3.

Rnd 15 2 Sl st, ch 3 (counts as 1 hdc and ch 1), 1 hdc in ch sp, ch 3, 1 sc in ch sp of Fan, ch 3, V-St in ch-1 sp, ch 3, 1 sc in ch sp of Fan, *ch 3, skip 3 dc and 1 sc, V-St in next sc, 1 dc in each of next 2 sts, Corner in ch sp, 1 dc in each of next 2 sts, V-St in next st, [ch 3, 1 sc in ch sp of Fan, ch 3, V-St in ch sp] 5 times, ch 3, 1 sc in ch sp of Fan; rep from *, ending last rep with [ch 3, 1 sc in ch sp of Fan, ch 3, V-St in ch sp] 3 times, ch 3, 1 sc in ch sp of Fan, ch 3. Join with sl st in 2nd ch of beg ch-3.

Rnds 16–18 Rep rnds 12–14 increasing number of st reps between [ ] as established by 1 on each rnd—352 sts.

Rnd 19 2 Sl st, ch 5, (counts as 1 hdc and ch 3), [1 sc in ch sp of Fan, ch 3, 1 hdc in next ch-1 sp, ch 3] 3 times, *1 sc in ch sp of Fan, ch 3, skip 3 dc and 1 sc,1 hdc in each of next 4 sts, Corner in ch sp, 1 hdc in each of next 4 sts, [ch 3, 1 sc in ch sp of Fan, ch 3, 1 hdc in next ch-1 sp] 7 times, ch 3; rep from *, ending last rep with [ch 3, 1 sc in Fan sp, ch 3, 1 hdc in next ch-1 sp] 4 times, ch 3. Join with sl st in 2nd ch of beg ch-5 – 316 sts.

Rnd 20 Ch 3 (counts as 1 dc), [3 dc in ch-3 sp, 1 dc in sc, 3 dc in ch-3 sp, 1 dc in hdc] 3 times, *6 dc, Corner in ch sp, 6 dc, [3 dc in ch sp, 1 dc in sc, 3 dc in ch-3 sp, 1 dc in hdc] 8 times; rep from *, ending last rep with [3 dc in ch sp, 1 dc in sc, 3 dc in ch-3 sp, 1 dc in hdc] 4 times, 3 dc in ch sp, 1 dc in sc, 3 dc in ch-3 sp. Join with sl st to top of beg ch-3—332 dc and ch-3 corner sts.

Eyelet Band

Rnd 21 Ch 4 (count as 1 dc and ch 1), [skip 1, 1 dc, ch 1] 15 times, *(1 dc, ch 1) 3 times in corner ch, 1 dc in first st, ch 1, [skip 1, 1 dc, ch 1] 39 times; rep from *, ending last rep with [skip 1, 1 dc, ch 1] 23 times. Join with sl st in 3rd ch of beg ch-4.

Rnd 22 Ch 3 (do not count), *BCdc over next 2 ch sps; rep from *, ending last rep with 1 dc in ch sp of beg ch-3, 1 dc in last ch of rnd behind previous st. Join with sl st to top of beg ch-3.

Rnd 23 Ch 4 (count as 1 dc and ch 1),

[skip 1, 1 dc, ch 1] 15 times,*(1 dc, ch 1) in each of next 4 corner sts, [skip 1, 1 dc, ch 1] 41 times; rep from *, ending last rep [skip 1, 1 dc, ch 1] 25 times. Join with sl st to 3rd ch of beg ch-4.

Rnd 24 Ch 3 (count as 1 dc), [1 dc in ch, 1 dc in dc] 16 times, *ch 3 for corner, [1 dc in ch, 1 dc in dc] 45 times; rep from *, ending last rep with [1 dc in ch, 1 dc in dc] 28 times, 1 dc in ch. Join with sl st to top of beg ch-3—372 dc and corner ch-3 sts. Fasten off.

Shell Band

With RS facing, attach MC in 51st st from right hand corner (do not count corner ch sts).

Rnd 25 Ch 3 (count as 1 dc), 2 dc in same st, [skip 2, 1 sc in next st, ch 5, skip 5, 1 sc in next st, skip 2, Shell in next st] 3 times, skip 2, *1 sc, ch 5, skip corner sp, 1 sc in next st, [skip 2, Shell in next st, skip 2, 1 sc in next st, ch 5, skip 5, 1 sc in next st] 7 times, skip 2, 5 dc in next st, skip 2, 1 sc in next st; rep from *, ending last rep with [skip 2, Shell in next st, skip 2, 1 sc in next st, ch 5, skip 5, 1 sc in next st] 4 times, skip 2, 2 dc in beg ch-3 sp. Join with sl st to top of beg ch-3.

Rnd 26 Ch 5, 1 sc in 5 ch sp, [ch 5, 1 sc in 3rd dc of Shell, ch 5, 1 sc in next ch sp] 3 times, *ch 5, 1 sc in same ch sp, [ch 5, 1 sc in 3rd dc of Shell, ch 5, 1 sc in next ch sp] 8 times, rep from *, ending last rep

with [ch 5, 1 sc in 3rd dc of Shell, ch 5, 1 sc in next ch sp] 4 times, ch 5. Join with sl st to 1st ch of beg ch-5.

Rnd 27 [Ch 5, 1 sc in ch sp, Shell in next sc, 1 sc in ch-5 sp] 4 times, *ch 5, 1 sc in same ch sp, [Shell in next sc, 1 sc in ch-5 sp, ch 5, 1 sc in ch sp] 9 times; rep from *, ending last rep with [Shell in next sc, 1 sc in ch-5 sp, ch 5, 1 sc in ch sp] 5 times. Join with sl st to 1st ch of beg ch-5.

Rnd 28 [Ch 5, 1 sc in 3rd dc of Shell, ch 5, 1 sc in ch sp] 4 times *ch 5, 1 sc in same ch sp, [ch 5, 1 sc in 3rd dc of Shell, ch 5, 1 sc in ch sp] 9 times; rep from *, ending last rep with [ch 5, 1 sc in 3rd dc of Shell, ch 5, 1 sc in ch sp] 5 times. Join with 1 sc in base ch of beg ch-5.

Rnd 29 Ch 3 (counts as 1 dc), 2 dc in same st, 1 sc in ch sp, ch 5, 1 sc in next ch sp, [Shell in next sc, 1 sc in next ch sp, ch 5, 1 sc in next ch sp] 3 times, *Shell in next sc, 1 sc in next ch sp, ch 5, 1 sc in same ch sp, [Shell in next sc, 1 sc in next ch sp, ch 5, 1 sc in next ch sp] 9 times; rep from *, ending last rep with [Shell in next sc, 1 sc in next ch sp, ch 5, 1 sc in next ch sp] 5 times, 2 dc in same st as beg ch-3. Join with sl st to 2nd ch of beg ch-3.

Rnd 30 [Ch 5, 1 sc in ch sp, ch 5, 1 sc in 3rd dc of Shell] 3 times, *ch 5, 1 sc in next ch sp, ch 5, 1 sc in same ch sp, [ch 5, 1 sc in 3rd dc of Shell, 1 sc in next ch sp, ch 5] 8 times; rep from *, ending last rep with [ch 5, 1 sc in 3rd dc of Shell, 1 sc in next ch sp, ch 5] 5 times. Join with 1 sc in base of ch-5.

Rnds 31–41 Rep rnds 27-30 twice, then rnds 27–29 once, increasing number of st reps between [ ] as established on each rnd.

Rnd 42 Ch 3, 1 sc in ch-5 sp [ch 3, 1 sc in 3rd dc of Shell, ch 3, 1 sc in next ch sp] 6 times, *ch 3, 1 sc in same ch sp, [ch 3, 1 sc in 3rd dc of Shell, ch 3, 1 sc in next ch sp] 14 times, rep from *, ending last rep with [ch 3, 1 sc in 3rd dc of Shell, ch 3, 1 sc in next ch sp] 7 times, ch 3, 1 sc in 3rd dc of Shell. Join with sl st to 1st ch of beg ch-3.

Rnd 43 Ch 3 (count as 1 dc), skip 1 sc, 3 dc in ch sp, [1 dc in sc, 3 dc in ch sp] 12 times, *1 dc in sc, (2 dc, ch 3, 2 dc) in corner ch, [1 dc in sc, 3 dc in ch sp] 28 times; rep from *, ending last rep with [1 dc in sc, 3 dc in ch sp] 15 times—480 sts. Join with sl st to top of beg ch-3.

Eyelet Band

Rnds 44–47 Rep rnds 21–24, increasing number of st reps between [ ] as established on each rnd —512 sts. Fasten off.

Ruffle

Rnd 48 With CC, 1 sc in each st around. Change to size G hook.

Rnd 49 Ch 3 (count as 1 sc and ch 2), skip 1 sc, *1 sc in next sc, ch 2, skip 1 sc; rep from * around. Join with sl st to 1st ch of beg ch-3.

Rnds 50–52 Ch 5 (count as 1 hdc and ch 3), *1 hdc in next hdc, ch 3; rep from * around. Join with sl st to 2nd ch of beg ch-5.

Rnd 53 Ch 6 (count as 1 hdc and ch 4), *1 hdc in next hdc, ch 4; rep from * around. Join with sl st to 2nd ch beg ch-6.

Rnd 54 Ch 7 (count as 1 hdc and ch 5), *1 hdc in next hdc, ch 5; rep from * around. Join with sl st to 2nd ch st of beg ch-7.

Rnd 55 Ch 8 (count as 1 sc and ch 7), *1 sc in next hdc, ch 7; rep from * around. Join with sl st to 1st ch st of beg ch-8. Fasten off.

FINISHING

Weave in loose ends. Steam lightly, pulling slightly to open Shell lace and pulling ruffle into points. Let dry. Thread ribbon through eyelet rows and tie into bows at corners as shown.

BUNDLER BLANKET

Pretty papoose

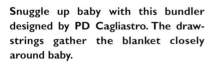

Snuggle up baby with this bundler designed by PD Cagliastro. The drawstrings gather the blanket closely around baby.

FINISHED MEASUREMENTS

■ 30"/76cm square

MATERIALS

■ 5 1.75oz/50g skeins (each approx 137yds/125m) of Filatura Di Crosa/ Tahki•Stacy Charles, Inc. *Zara* (merino wool) in #1461 burgundy (A) **③**

■ 3 skeins each in #1472 light blue (B) and #1499 blue (C)

■ Size I/9 (5.5mm) and N/13 (10mm) crochet hooks *or sizes to obtain gauge*

■ Yarn needle

GAUGE

19 sts and 14 rows to 4"/10cm over sc pat using size I/9 (5.5mm) crochet hook.
Take time to check gauge.

Notes

1 Unless otherwise indicated, work through FL only and single crochet throughout.

2 Join new color by working st in old color to last 2 lps; leaving 6"/15cm tail, complete st by drawing new color through 2 lps and continue with new color.

3 Carry unused yarn across top of row and work over with new color.

BLANKET

With smaller hook and A, ch 131.

Row 1 (RS) 1 Sc in 2nd ch from hook and in each ch across—130A sc. Turn.

Row 2 Ch 1, 1 sc in each sc across. Turn.

Color Block #1

Row 3 Ch 1, 5A, *4B, 4A; rep from *, end last rep with 1A. Turn.

Row 4 Ch 1, 2A, *4B, 4A; rep from *, end last rep with 4A. Turn.

Row 5 Ch 1, 3A, *4B, 4A; rep from *, end last rep with 3A. Turn.

Row 6 Ch 1, 2A, *4B, 4A; rep from * to end. Turn.

Row 7 Ch 1, 5A, *4B, 4A; rep from *, end last rep with 1A. Turn.

Rows 8 and 9 Ch 1, with A, 1 sc in each sc across. Turn.

Rows 10 and 11 Ch 1, with B, 1 sc in each sc across. Turn.

Color Block #2

Rows 12–14 Ch 1, 5A, *12B, 4A; rep from *, end last rep with 1A. Turn.

Rows 15, 16, 19 and 20 Ch 1, with A, 1 sc in each sc across. Turn.

Rows 17 and 18 Ch 1, with B, 1 sc in each sc across. Turn.

Rows 21–24 Ch 1, with C, 1 sc in each sc across. Turn.

Color Block #3

Row 25 Ch 1, 9A, 13C, 18A, 7C, 11A, 14C, 11A, 7C, 18A, 13C, 9A. Turn.

Row 26 Ch 1, 10A, 11C, 20A, 5C, 13A,

12C, 13A, 5C, 20A, 11C, 10A. Turn.

Row 27 Ch 1, 11A, 9C, 22A, 3C, 15A, 10C, 15A, 3C, 22A, 9C, 11A. Turn.

Row 28 Ch 1, 12A, 7C, 24A, 1C, 17A, 8C, 17A, 1C, 24A, 7C, 12A. Turn.

Mark end of row for attaching tie.

Row 29 Ch 1, 13A, 5C, 44A, 6C, 44A, 5C, 13A. Turn.

Row 30 Ch 1, 14A, 3C, 46A, 4C, 46A, 3C, 14A. Turn.

Row 31 Ch 1, 15A, 1C, 48A, 2C, 48A, 1C, 15A. Turn.

Rows 32 and 33 Ch 1, with A, 1 sc in each sc across. Turn.

Rows 34–44 Ch 1, with C, 1 sc in each sc across. Turn.

Rows 45 and 46 Ch 1, with A, 1 sc in each sc across. Turn.

Rows 47–58 Ch 1, with B, 1 sc in each sc across. Turn.

Mark end of row for attaching tie.

Rows 59–71 Ch 1, with A, 1 sc in each sc across. Turn.

Rows 72–82 Ch 1, with B, 1 sc in each sc across. Turn.

Rows 83–86 Ch 1, with A, 1 sc in each sc across. Turn.

Rows 87 and 88 Ch 1, with C, 1 sc in each sc across. Turn.

Color Block #4

Rows 89 and 92 Ch 1, *5C, 5A; rep from * to end. Turn.

Rows 90 and 91 Ch 1, *5A, 5C; rep from * to end. Turn.

Rows 93 and 94 Ch 1, with C, 1 sc in each sc across. Turn.

Rows 95 and 96 Ch 1, with A, 1 sc in each sc across. Do not fasten off. Turn.

TOP EDGE SHAPING

Row 97 Sl st 10 sts from edge, 1 sc in next and each st across, leaving last 10 sts unworked. Turn.

Row 98 Sl st in first 6 sts, 1 sc in next and each st across, leaving last 6 sts unworked. Turn.

Row 99 Sl st in first 3 sts, 1 sc in next and each st across, leaving last 3 sts unworked. Turn.

Rows 100–103 Sl st in first 5 sts, 1 sc in next and each st across, leaving last 5 sts unworked. Turn.

Rows 104–107 Sl st in first 4 sts, 1 sc in next and each st across, leaving last 4 sts unworked. Fasten off.

SHELL EDGING

Note Sc is worked through both lps.

Rnd 1 (RS) With A, sc evenly around sides and top edges only, with 3 sc in each corner. Fasten off.

Rnd 2 With C, sc evenly along bottom and around sides and top edges, with 3 sc in each corner—512 sc. Join with sl st to first sc.

Rnd 3 ** *3 sc, ch 2, skip 2 sc; rep from * until 2 sts before corner, [1 sc, ch 2, skip

1 sc] twice at corner; rep from ** around.
Join with sl st to first sc.

Rnd 4 Ch 3 (counts as 1 dc), 5 dc in ch-2
sp, *1 sc in center 3-sc group, 6 dc in ch-
2 sp; rep from * around. Join with sl st to
top of ch-3.

Rnd 5 With A, ch 1, *1 sc through FL of
each dc, 1 sc through both lps of each sc;
rep from * around. Join with sl st to first
sc. Fasten off.

FINISHING
Weave in ends.

DRAWSTRINGS
(make 2)
With larger hook and 1 strand of each
color, ch 131. Fasten off.

(make 4)
With larger hook and 1 strand of each
color, ch 41. Fasten off.

From RS of blanket, weave long drawstrings around top and bottom beg from
center 6-dc group. Tie knot at ends.

Knot ends of short drawstrings. Sew 2
indicated by markers above. Sew rem 2
along same row 4"/10cm away from edging on opposite end.

USING BUNDLER
1 Use as regular blanket.
2 Pull drawstring at bottom and tie.
Overlap sides and tie. Gently pull drawstring at top around baby's head and tie.

BUNNY BLANKET

Hop to it

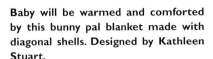

Baby will be warmed and comforted by this bunny pal blanket made with diagonal shells. Designed by Kathleen Stuart.

FINISHED MEASUREMENTS
▦ Approx 34"/86.5cm square

MATERIALS
▦ 3 8oz/227g skeins (each approx 500yds/457m) of Lorna's Laces *Fisherman* (wool) in #24 happy valley (MC) 🔢
▦ 1 skein in #29ns pale pink (CC)
▦ 1 yd/1m black worsted weight yarn
▦ Size J/10 (6mm) crochet hook *or size to obtain gauge*
▦ Polyester fiberfill
▦ Yarn needle

GAUGE
14 sts and 9 rows to 4"/10cm over pat using size J/10 (6mm) crochet hook.
Take time to check gauge.

STITCH GLOSSARY
Sc2tog (over 2 sts) [Draw lp in next st] twice, yo and through all 3 lps.

BUNNY
Head
Note Worked in spiral—do not join rnds. Mark first st of each rnd.
With MC, ch 2.

Rnd 1 6 sc in 2nd ch from hook—6 sc.
Rnd 2 2 sc in each st around—12 sc.
Rnd 3 *1 sc in next st, 2 sc in next st; rep from * around—18 sc.
Rnds 4–6 1 sc in each st around—18 sc.
Rnd 7 In BL only, *1 sc in each of next 2 sts, 2 sc in next st; rep from * around— 24 sc.
Rnd 8 *1 sc in each of next 3 sts, 2 sc in next st; rep from * around—30 sc.
Rnd 9 *1 sc in each of next 4 sts, 2 sc in next st; rep from * around—36 sc.
Rnd 10 *1 sc in each of next 5 sts, 2 sc in next st; rep from * around—42 sc.
Rnd 11 *1 sc in each of next 6 sts, 2 sc in next st; rep from * around—48 sc.
Rnds 12–15 1 sc in each st around—48 sc.
Rnd 16 *1 sc in each of next 6 sts, sc2tog; rep from * around—42 sc.
Rnd 17 *1 sc in each of next 5 sts, sc2tog; rep from * around—36 sc.
Rnd 18 *1 sc in each of next 4 sts, sc2tog; rep from * around—30 sc.
Rnd 19 *1 sc in each of next 3 sts, sc2tog; rep from * around—24 sc. Mark rnd.
Rnd 20 In BL only, *1 sc in each of next 2 sts, sc2tog; rep from * around—18 sc. Stuff with fiberfill.
Rnd 21 *1 sc in next st, sc2tog; rep from * around—12 sc.
Rnd 22 Sc2tog around—6 sc.
Stuff to complete. Sew to close.

Ears

(make 2)

Note Join at the end of each rnd. You will alternate starting rounds with MC and CC. With MC, ch 2.

Rnd 1 6 sc in 2nd ch from hook. Join CC (do not cut MC)—6 sts. Join with sl st to first sc. Turn.

Rnd 2 With CC, ch 1, 1 sc in next st, 2 sc in next st; with MC, *1 sc in next st, 2 sc in next st; rep from * around—3CC and 6MC sts. Join with sl st to first sc. Turn.

Rnd 3 With MC, ch 1, 1 sc in each of next 2 sts, 2 sc in next st, 1 sc in each of next 2 sts; with CC, 2 sc in next st, 1 sc in each of next 2 sts, 2 sc in last st—6CC and 6MC sts. Join with sl st to first sc. Turn.

Rnd 4 With CC, ch 1, 1 sc in each of next 3 sts, 2 sc in next st, 1 sc in each of next 2 sts; with MC, 1 sc in next st, 2 sc in next st, 1 sc in each of next 3 sts, 2 sc in last st—7CC and 8 MC sts. Join with sl st to first sc. Turn.

Rnd 5 With MC, ch 1, 1 sc in each of next 4 sts, 2 sc in next st, 1 sc in each of next 3 sts; with CC, 1 sc in next st, 2 sc in next st, 1 sc in each of next 4 sts, 2 sc in last st—9CC and 9MC sts. Join with sl st to first sc. Turn.

Rnd 6 With CC, ch 1, 1 sc in each of next 9 sts; with MC, 1 sc in each of next 9 sts—9CC and 9MC sts. Join with sl st to first sc. Turn.

Rnd 7 With MC, ch 1, 1 sc in each of next 9 sts; with CC, 1 sc in each of next 9 sts—9CC and 9MC sts. Join with sl st to first sc. Turn.

Rnds 8–23 Rep rnds 6 and 7.

Rnd 24 With CC, ch 1, [1 sc in next st, sc2tog] 3 times; with MC, [1 sc in next st, sc2tog] 3 times—6CC and 6MC sts. Join with sl st to first sc. Turn.

Rnd 25 With MC, ch 1, sc2tog around. Join with sl st to first sc.

Fasten off, leaving 10"/25.5cm tail for sewing.

With MC, ch 54. Connect bunny head by working through FL of rnd 19 of head; flatten round to work through two sts at a time (start with first and last sts tog), 1 sc in each of next 9 sts, ch 54.

Row 1 Skip 2 ch (counts as 1 sc), (1 hdc, 1 dc) in next ch, *skip 2 ch, (1 sc, 1 hdc, 1 dc) in next ch; rep from * across to last 3 ch, skip 2 ch, 1 sc in last ch (the sc connecting the head counts as ch st). Turn.

Row 2 Ch 1, (1 hdc, 1 dc) in first sc, *skip (1 dc, 1 hdc), (1 sc, 1 hdc, 1 dc) in next sc; rep from * to last 3 sts, skip (1 dc, 1 hdc), 1 sc in top of t-ch. Turn.

Rows 3–77 Rep row 2 until blanket measures 34"/86.5cm from beg. Fasten off.

Weave in ends.

Ears

Flatten and sew, with pink side toward head, to sides near top between rnds 14 and 17.

Embroidery

With CC, embroider nose with satin stitch starting at center of face over rnds 2 and 3. With CC, embroider mouth with straight stitch from bottom of nose and near rnd 2. With black, embroider eyes with satin stitch starting on rnd 7, working over rnds 7 and 8 and near center with 1 to 2 sts in between eyes.

Join as you go with tricolor granny squares and a double crochet shell edging. Designed by Marty Miller.

FINISHED MEASUREMENTS

■ 30"/76cm square

MATERIALS

■ 5 1.75oz/50g skeins (each approx 84yds/77m) of Mission Falls *1824 Cotton* (cotton) in #301 fennell (A) (**4**)

■ 3 skeins each in #305 lemon grass (B) and in #209 maize (C)

■ Size H/8 (5mm) crochet hook *or size to obtain gauge*

■ Yarn needle

GAUGE

Each square approx 4"/10cm x 4"/10cm using size H/8 (5mm) crochet hook.
Take time to check gauge.

Notes

1 Join new color by working st in old color to last 2 lps; leaving 6"/15cm tail, complete st by drawing new color through 2 lps and continue with new color.

2 Second and subsequent squares are completed and joined on rnd 3.

STITCH GLOSSARY

Sc2tog (over 2 sts) [Draw lp in next st] twice, yo and draw through all 3 lps.

SQUARE I

(make 1)

With B, ch 4. Join with sl st to first ch to form ring.

Rnd I Ch 3 (counts as 1 dc), 2 dc in ring, *ch 1, 3 dc in ring; rep from * twice, end ch 1. Join with a sl st to top of beg ch-3. Fasten off.

Rnd 2 Join B in ch-1 sp, ch 3 (counts as 1 dc), (2 dc, ch 1, 3 dc) in same ch-1 sp, *ch 1, (3 dc, ch 1, 3 dc) in next ch-1 sp; rep from * twice, end ch 1. Join with sl st to top of beg ch-3. Fasten off.

Rnd 3 Join A in next corner ch-1 sp, ch 3, (2 dc, ch 1, 3 dc) in same sp, *ch 1, 3 dc in next ch-1 space, ch 1, (3 dc, ch 1, 3 dc) in corner ch-1 sp; rep from * twice, end ch 1, 3 dc in next ch-1 sp, ch 1. Join with sl st to top of beg ch-3. Fasten off.

SQUARE 2

(make 48)

Rnd I Rep rnd 1 of Square 1.

Rnd 2 Rep rnd 2 of Square 1.

Rnd 3 (Joining) Rep rnd 3 of Square 1 to point of beg to join to Square 1.

For corner ch-1 sp, work (3 dc in Square 2, 1 sc in corner ch-1 sp of Square 1, 3 dc in same corner of Square 2).

For sides, work (1 sc in next ch-1 sp of Square 1, 3 dc in next ch-1 sp of Square 2, 1 sc in next ch-1 sp of Square 1).

Finish non-joining sides same as rnd 3 of Square 1. Fasten off.

Squares 3–7 will be joined on one side only, repeating joining for Squares 1 and 2. Squares 8–49 will be joined on two sides. When joining 4 corners tog, the joining sc in the corner of the last square will be worked in the opposite corner square, not the adjacent one.

BORDER

Join B to corner ch-1 sp, ch 1, 1 sc in same sp, *[skip 1 dc, (3dc, ch 1, 3dc) in next dc, 1 sc in next ch-1 sp] twice, skip 1 dc, (3dc, ch 1, 3dc) in next dc, sc2tog in next two adjacent corner ch-1 sps; rep from * around working sc2tog in adjacent corner ch-1 sps, and 1 sc in the 4 corner ch-1 sps, end last rep with omit sc2tog. Join with sl st to first sc. Fasten off.

FINISHING

Weave in ends.

49	48	47	46	45	44	43
42	41	40	39	38	37	36
35	34	33	32	31	30	29
28	27	26	25	24	23	22
21	20	19	18	17	16	15
14	13	12	11	10	9	8
7	6	5	4	3	2	1

FLORAL MEDALLION BLANKET

Pumpkin spice

Flowers surround baby with Linda Medina's medallion design. Crab stitch edging completes the blanket.

FINISHED MEASUREMENTS

■ 28½"/72.5cm square

MATERIALS

■ 6 1.75oz/50g skeins (each approx 104yds/95m) of Artyarns *Supermerino* (merino wool) in #201 pumpkin (MC) 🔟

■ 3 skeins in #103 yellow multis (CC)
■ Size G/6 (4mm) crochet hook *or size to obtain gauge*
■ Yarn needle
■ Markers

GAUGE

One floral square approx 3½"/9.5cm x 3½"/9.5cm using size G/6 (4mm) crochet hook. *Take time to check gauge.*

STITCH GLOSSARY

Dc3tog Cluster (Dc3togCL) [Yo and draw lp, yo and draw through 2 lps] 3 times in same st, yo and through all 4 lps.
Dc4tog Cluster (Dc4togCL) [Yo and draw lp, yo and draw through 2 lps] 4 times in same st, yo and through all 5 lps.

SQUARE

(make 49)
With CC, ch 6. Join with sl st to form ring.

Rnd 1 (RS) Ch 5 (counts as 1 dc and ch 2), [1 dc in ring, ch 2] 7 times. Join with sl st to 3rd ch of beg ch-5—8 sps.

Rnd 2 Sl st into first ch-sp, ch 3, Dc3togCL in same ch-sp, [ch 5, Dc4togCL in next ch-sp] 7 times, end ch 5. Join with sl st to top of first cluster. Fasten off. Join MC in same st.

Rnd 3 With MC, ch 1, 1 sc in same st, *ch 2, working over ch-5 sp, 1 dc in dc of 1st rnd, ch 2, 1 sc in top of next cluster; rep from * around, ending last rep with 1 dc in dc of 1st rnd, ch 2. Join with sl st to first sc.

Rnd 4 Sl st into next ch-sp, ch 1, 1 sc in same ch-sp, *ch 3, 1 sc in next ch-sp; rep from * around, ending last rep with ch 3. Join with sl st to first sc.

Rnd 5 Sl st into next ch-sp, ch 3 (counts as 1 dc), (1 dc, ch 2, 2 dc) in same ch-sp, *ch 2, 1 sc in next ch-sp, [ch 3, 1 sc in next ch-sp] twice, ch 2**, (2 dc, ch 2, 2dc) in next ch-sp—for Corner; rep from * around, ending last rep at **. Join with sl st to top of beg ch-3. Fasten off.
Arrange squares 7 x 7 and join together.

EDGING

With RS facing, join MC in 1st dc after ch-2 sp in corner.

Rnd 1 Ch 1, *1 sc in each of first 2 dc, 1 sc in next ch-2 sp, 1 sc in next sc, 1 sc in next ch-2 space, [1 sc in next sc, 1 sc in next ch-3 sp] twice, 1 sc in each of next 2 dc, 1 sc in ch-2 sp—12 sc along block edge; rep from * to corner, 3 sc in ch-2 sp, rep from * around. Join with sl st to first sc. Marker center sc of each corner.

Rnd 2 Ch 1, 1 sc in first and in next 2 sc, *join CC, 1 sc in each sc across to 4 sc before corner marker, join MC, 1 sc in each of next 4 sc, 3 sc in marked corner sc, 1 sc in each of next 4 sc; rep from * around, ending last rep with 3 sc in marked corner sc, 1 sc in last sc. Join sl st to first sc. Mark center sc of each corner.

Rnd 3 Ch 3 (counts as 1 dc), *1 dc in each sc, 3 dc in marked corner sc; rep from * around. Join with sl st to top of beg ch-3.

Rnd 4 Ch 1, working from left to right, 1 sc in last dc from previous rnd and in each dc around—reverse sc. Join with sl st to first reverse sc. Fasten off.

FINISHING

Weave in ends and block lightly.

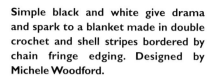

Simple black and white give drama and spark to a blanket made in double crochet and shell stripes bordered by chain fringe edging. Designed by Michele Woodford.

FINISHED MEASUREMENTS
- 33"/84cm wide x 37½"/95.5cm long, including chain fringe

MATERIALS
- 5 5oz/140g skeins (each approx 236yds/212m) of Lion Brand Yarn *Lion Cotton* (cotton) in #153 black (MC) [4]
- 1 skein in #100 white (CC)
- Size G/6 (4mm) and H/8 (5mm) crochet hooks *or sizes to obtain gauge*
- Yarn needle

GAUGE
15 sts and 8 rows to 4"/10cm over dc using size G/6 (4mm) crochet hook. *Take time to check gauge.*

STITCH GLOSSARY
Shell 7 Dc in same st.

Front Post Double Crochet (FPdc) Yo and insert hook from front to back to front around post of st in row below; complete as a dc.

Back Post Double Crochet (BPdc) Yo and insert hook from back to front to back around post of st in row below; complete as a dc.

BLANKET
With MC and larger hook, ch 122. Change to smaller hook.

Row 1 (RS) 1 Dc in 4th ch from hook (ch 3 counts as 1 dc), 1 dc in each ch across—120 dc. Turn.

Rows 2 and 3 Ch 3 (counts as 1 dc), skip first dc, 1 dc in each dc across, ending with dc in top of ch-3. Turn.

Row 4 Ch 2, 1 sc in each of next 3 dc, *ch 3, skip 1 dc, 1 sc in each of next 7 dc; rep from *, ending last rep with 1 sc in last 3 dc, 1 sc in top of ch-3. Join CC. Turn.

Row 5 With CC, ch 3, skip 4 sc, *Shell in ch-3 sp, ch 1, skip 3 sc, 1 sc in next sc, ch 1; rep from *, ending last rep with 1 sc in top of ch-2. Join MC. Turn.

Row 6 With MC, ch 7, *1 sc in 4th dc of Shell, ch 3, FPdc around sc, ch 3; rep from *, ending last rep with 1 dc in first ch of ch-3. Turn.

Row 7 Ch 3, *3 dc in ch-3 sp, 1 dc in sc, 3 dc in next ch-3 sp, 1 dc in dc; rep from *, across, ending last rep with 3 dc in ch-7 loop—120 dc. Turn.

Rows 8–10 Rep row 2.

Rows 11 and 12 Rep rows 4 and 5.

Row 13 With MC, ch 7, *1 sc in 4th dc of Shell, ch 3, BPdc around sc, ch 3; rep from *, ending with 1 dc in first ch of ch-3. Turn.

Rows 14–17 Rep rows 7–10.

Rep rows 4–17 four times, Rep rows 4–9 once. Fasten off.

Edging

With RS facing, join MC at corner, ch 2 (counts as 1 hdc), 1 hdc in corner, *hdc evenly along one edge, 3 hdc in next corner; rep from * around blanket, ending last rep with 1 hdc in beg corner. Join with sl st to top of beg ch-2. Do not fasten off. Turn to work along top (or bottom) edge.

Chain Fringe

*Ch 22, 1 sc in same st as first ch, 1 sc in each of next 3 sts; rep from *, ending with 1 sc in next st, ch 22, 1 sc in same st as first ch. Fasten off.

Join MC in corner at opposite edge and rep chain fringe.

Weave in ends. Block lightly if desired.

CLOVER BLANKET

Blues snooze

Love (and luck!) are woven into this design of clover leaves. 4-leaf clusters are embedded in the blanket, which is then trimmed with a border of 3-leaf clovers. Designed by Lidia Karabinech.

FINISHED MEASUREMENTS

■ 30"/76cm wide x 27"/68.5cm long

MATERIALS

■ 7 1.75oz/50g skeins (each approx 110yds/101m) of Alchemy Yarns of Transformation *Synchronicity* (silk/merino wool) in #92w moonstone (MC) ▣

■ 2 skeins in #82w jan boy's sapphire (CC)

■ Size G/6 (4mm) crochet hook *or size to obtain gauge*

■ Yarn needle

GAUGE

19 sts and 8½ rows to 4"/10cm over Dc3CL pat using size G/6 (4mm) crochet hook. *Take time to check gauge.*

STITCH GLOSSARY

Dc3Cluster (Dc3CL) [Yo and draw lp, yo and draw through 2 lps] 3 times in next st, yo and through all 4 lps.

Tr2Cluster (Tr2CL) [Yo twice and draw lp, (yo and draw through 2 lps) twice] 2 times in next st, yo and draw through all 3 lps.

Tr3Cluster (Tr3CL) [Yo twice and draw lp, (yo and draw through 2 lps) twice] 3 times in next st, yo and draw through all 4 lps.

BLANKET

With MC, ch 129.

Row 1 1 Dc in 4th ch from hook, 1 dc in each of next 4 ch, *ch 3, Dc3CL in next ch, skip 3 ch, Dc3CL in next ch, ch 3, 1 dc in each of next 5 ch; rep from *, ending with 1 dc in last ch.

Row 2 Ch 3 (counts as 1 dc), *1 dc in each of next 5 dc, (Dc3CL, ch 3, Dc3CL) in st between 2 Clusters from previous row; rep from *, ending last rep with 1 dc in last 5 dc, 1 dc in top of beg ch-3.

Row 3 Ch 6 (counts as 1 dc and ch 3), Dc3CL in next dc, skip 3 dc, Dc3CL in next dc, ch 3, *1 dc in top of dc Cluster, 3 dc in ch-3 sp, 1 dc in top of dc Cluster, ch 3, Dc3CL in next dc, skip 3 dc, Dc3CL in next dc, ch 3; rep from *, ending with 1 dc in top of ch-3.

Row 4 Ch 3 (counts as 1 dc), *(Dc3CL, ch 3, Dc3CL) in st between 2 Clusters from previous row, 1 dc in each of next 5 dc; rep from *, ending with (Dc3CL, ch 3, Dc3CL) in st between 2 Clusters from previous row, 1 dc in top of ch-3.

Row 5 Ch 3 (counts as 1 dc), *1 dc in top of dc Cluster, 3 dc in ch-3 sp, 1 dc in top of dc Cluster, ch 3, Dc3CL in next dc, skip 3 dc, Dc3CL in next dc, ch 3; rep from *, ending with 1 dc in top of dc Cluster, 3 dc in ch-3 sp, 1 dc in top of dc Cluster, 1 dc in top of ch-3.

Row 6 Ch 3 (counts as 1 dc), *1 dc in each of next 5 dc, (Dc3CL, ch 3, Dc3CL) in st between 2 Clusters from previous row; repeat from *, ending with 1 dc in each of next 5 dc, 1 dc in top of ch-3.

Rep rows 3–6 10 times. Fasten off.

BORDER

Join CC to first dc at side edge after corner.
Rnd 1 Ch 1, [*(1 sc in dc, 1 sc in top of dc Cluster, ch 3, 1 sc in top of next Cluster, 1 sc in next dc, ch 3); rep from *, ending last rep with ch 5 for corner, **(1 sc in each of next 2 sts, ch 3); rep from **, ending last rep with ch 5 for corner]; rep between [ ] once more. Join with sl st to first sc.
Rnd 2 Sl st to ch-3 sp, ch 4 (counts as 1 tr), Tr2CL in ch-3 sp, *(ch 8, in 5th ch from hook work (1 dc, ch 4, sl st in ch, [ch 4, 1 dc, ch 4, sl st in ch] twice, ch 3), Tr3CL in same ch-3 sp, ch 1, Tr3CL in next ch-3 sp; rep from *, ending last rep with Tr3CL in corner ch-5 sp, [rep between ( ) once, Tr3CL in same ch-5 sp] twice, ch 1, Tr3CL in next ch-3 sp; rep from * around, ending last rep with [rep between ( ) once, Tr3CL in same ch-5 sp] twice, ch 1. Join with sl st to first tr. Fasten off.

FINISHING

Weave in ends.

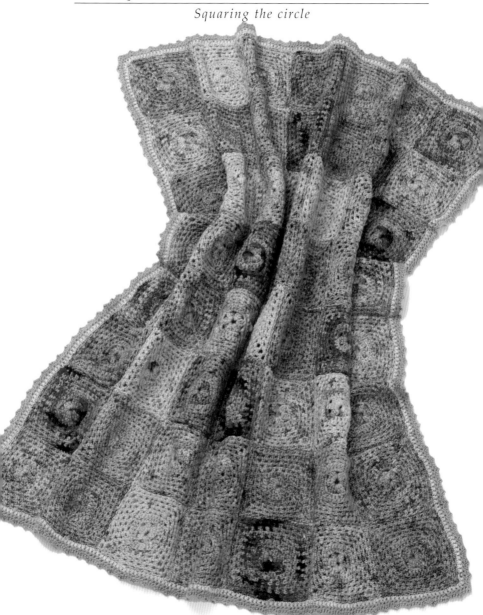

Eight different variegated colorways complement each other beautifully in this granny square blanket designed by Maie Landra. The single crochet border boasts picot edging.

FINISHED MEASUREMENTS
■ 29"/73.5cm wide x 33"/84cm long

MATERIALS
■ 2 1.75oz/50g hanks (each approx 114yds/104m) of Koigu Wool Designs *Kersti* (merino wool) each in #K506A (C1), #K121L (C2), #K822 (C3), #K402 (C4), #K432L (C5), #K809L (C6), #K103 (C7), #K207 (C8) **3**
■ 1 skein each in #K2231 (C9), #K2163 (C10), #K2181 (C11)
■ Size F/5 (3.75mm) crochet hook *or size to obtain gauge*
■ Yarn needle

GAUGE
Each square = 4"/10cm x 4"/10cm using size F/5 (3.75mm) crochet hook.
Take time to check gauge.

STITCH GLOSSARY
Dc2tog (over 2 sts) [Yo and draw lp in next st, yo and draw through 2 lps] twice, yo and draw through all 3 lps on hook.
Dc3tog (over 3 sts) [Yo and draw lp in next st, yo and draw through 2 lps] 3 times, yo and draw through all 4 lps on hook.

SQUARE
(make 7 each using C1–C8)
Ch 5. Join with sl st to form ring.
Rnd 1 (RS) Ch 3, Dc2tog in ring, *ch 3, Dc3tog in ring; rep from * 5 times, ch 3. Join with sl st to top of beg dc2tog.
Rnd 2 Ch 1, 1 sc first st, *3 sc in ch sp, 1 sc in next st; rep from * around, ending last rep with 3 sc in ch sp—24 sts. Join with sl st to first sc.
Rnd 3 Working in BL, ch 1, 1 sc in first and each of next 4 sts, *(1 sc, ch 1, 1 sc) in next st—for corner, 1 sc in each of next 5 sts; rep from * around, ending last rep with (1 sc, ch 1, 1sc) in last st. Join with sl st to first sc.
Rnd 4 Ch 3 (counts as 1 hdc and ch 1), [skip 1, 1 hdc, ch 1] twice, skip 1, *(1 hdc, ch 1, 1 hdc) in corner ch sp, ch 1, [skip 1, 1 hdc, ch 1] 3 times; rep from * around, ending last rep with (1 hdc, ch 1, 1 hdc) in corner ch sp, ch 1. Join with sl st to 2nd ch of beg ch-3.
Rnd 5 Sl st in ch sp, ch 3 (counts as 1 hdc and ch 1), [skip 1 st, 1 hdc in next sp, ch 1] twice, *(1 hdc, ch 1, 1 hdc) in corner ch sp, ch 1, [skip 1 st, 1 hdc in next sp, ch 1] 4 times; rep from * around, ending last rep with [skip 1 st, 1 hdc in next sp, ch 1] once. Join with sl st to 2nd ch of beg ch-3.
Rnd 6 Sl st in ch sp, ch 3 (counts as 1 hdc and ch 1), [skip 1 st, 1 hdc in next sp, ch 1] twice, *(1 hdc, ch 1, 1 hdc) in corner ch sp, ch 1, [skip 1 st, 1 hdc in next sp, ch 1]

5 times; rep from *, ending last rep with [skip 1 st, 1 hdc in next sp, ch 1] twice. Join with sl st to 2nd ch of beg ch-3.

Rnd 7 Sl st in ch sp, ch 3 (counts as 1 hdc and ch 1), [skip 1 st, 1 hdc in next sp, ch 1] twice, *(1 hdc, ch 2, 1 hdc) in corner ch sp, ch 1, [skip 1 st, 1 hdc in next sp, ch 1] 6 times; rep from *, ending last rep with [skip 1 st, 1 hdc in next sp, ch 1] 3 times. Join with sl st to 2nd ch of beg ch-3.

Rnd 8 Sl st in ch sp, ch 3 (counts as 1 hdc and ch 1), [skip 1 st, 1 hdc in next sp, ch 1] twice, *(1 hdc, ch 2, 1 hdc) in corner ch sp, ch 1, [skip 1 st, 1 hdc in next sp, ch 1] 7 times; rep from *, ending last rep with [skip 1 st, 1 hdc in next sp, ch 1] 4 times.

Join with sl st to 2nd ch of beg ch-3. Fasten off.

FINISHING

Arrange squares according to diagram and join squares with sl st.

EDGING

Rnd 1 With C11, ch 1, 1 sc evenly around with 3 sc in each corner. Join with sl st to first sc. Fasten off.

Rnd 2 With C10, rep rnd 1.

Rnd 3 With C9, *1 sc in next 3 sc, ch 3, sl st in same st as last sc; rep from * around. Join with sl st to first sc. Fasten off. Weave in ends.

C2	C7	C6	C8	C3	C5	C7
C1	C8	C5	C1	C7	C8	C6
C5	C3	C4	C6	C2	C3	C2
C4	C6	C2	C3	C4	C1	C5
C1	C8	C1	C5	C6	C7	C8
C6	C4	C3	C7	C4	C3	C2
C7	C2	C5	C6	C8	C5	C4
C4	C1	C8	C2	C7	C3	C1

#K121L	#K103	#K809L	#K207	#K822	#K432L	#K103
#K506A	#K207	#K432L	#K506A	#K103	#K207	#K809L
#K432L	#K822	#K402	#K809L	#K121L	#K822	#K121L
#K402	#K809L	#K121L	#K822	#K402	#K506A	#K432L
#K506A	#K207	#K506A	#K432L	#K809L	#K103	#K207
#K809L	#K402	#K822	#K103	#K402	#K822	#K121L
#K103	#K121L	#K432L	#K809L	#K207	#K432L	#K402
#K402	#K506A	#K207	#K121L	#K103	#K822	#K506A

WOVEN BLANKET
Green piece

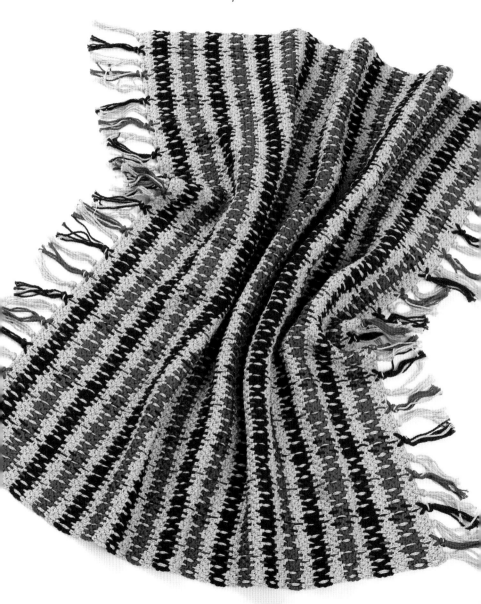

Horizontal stripes in double crochet background set the stage for a woven, textured design by Jennifer Appleby.

FINISHED MEASUREMENTS

■ 32"/81.5cm wide x 34"/86.5cm long

MATERIALS

■ 4 3.5oz/100g skeins (each approx 205yds/186m) of Classic Elite Yarns Provence (mercerized cotton) in #2681 bright chartreuse (MC) ⓷

■ 2 skeins each in #2610 marine (A) and #2657 de nimes blue (B)

■ Size G/6 (4mm) crochet hook *or size to obtain gauge*

■ Yarn needle

GAUGE

14 sts and 10½ rows to 4"/10cm over post-weaved dc using size G/6 (4mm) crochet hook. *Take time to check gauge.*

Note

Join new color at end of row by working st in old color to last 2 lps; leaving 6"/15cm tail, complete st by drawing new color through 2 lps and continue with new color.

BACKGROUND

With MC, ch 114.

Row 1 (RS) 1 Dc in 4th ch from hook, 1 dc in each ch to end—112 dc. Turn.

Row 2 Ch 3 (counts as 1 dc), 1 dc in next and in each st to end. Turn.

Rows 3 and 4 With A, rep row 2.

Rows 5 and 6 With MC, rep row 2.

Rows 7 and 8 With B, rep row 2.

Rows 9 and 10 With MC, rep row 2.

Rep rows 3–10, 8 times. Fasten off. Weave in ends.

WEAVING

Cut yarn lengths of 55"/139.5cm in each color, and use 2 strands tog for each lengthwise woven row.

Vertical Row 1 With MC and RS facing, weave strands vertically through spaces between first and second dc. Beg with needle going DOWN from RS to WS through first sp, and coming UP from WS to RS in sp of row above, leaving approx equal amounts of fringe at top and bottom.

Vertical Row 2 With MC and RS facing, weave strands vertically through spaces between first and second dc. Beg with needle coming UP from WS to RS through first sp, and going DOWN from RS to WS in sp of row above, leaving approx equal amounts of fringe at top and bottom.

Rep vertical rows 1 and 2 for alternating weaving pat and continue in the following color sequence and yarn combination.

Row 3 2 strands MC.

Row 4 2 strands A.

Row 5 1 strand MC + 1 strand A.

Row 6 2 strands A.

Rows 7–9 2 strands MC.

Row 10 2 strands B.

Row 11 1 strand MC + 1 strand B.

Row 12 2 strands B.

Rows 13–15 2 strands MC.

Rep rows 4–15.

FINISHING

Pull gently on ends of fringe for each vertical row to even out weaving. Block blanket to finished measurements.

FRINGE

Knot 6 strands from first 3 vertical rows at each end. Continue knotting 6 strands from 3 vertical rows at each end all the way across. Trim fringe to 3"/7.5cm from blanket edge (including knot).

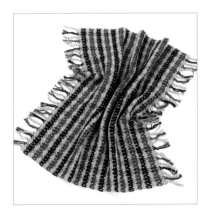

■■■□

Tunisian crochet, also called afghan stitch, is made with a hook that's a cross between a knitting needle and crochet hook. This is the backdrop for Noreen Crone-Findlay's stars-in-the-night intarsia. Other stars and moons are appliquéd.

FINISHED MEASUREMENTS

▨ 29"/73.5cm wide x 30"/76cm long

MATERIALS

▨ 5 3oz/85g skeins (each approx 826yds/755m) of Caron International *Simply Soft Shadows* (acrylic) in #5 soft merino (MC) (4)
▨ 2 skeins in #1 pearl frost (A)
▨ 1 6oz/454g skein (approx 153yds/140m) of Caron International *One Pound* (100% acrylic) in #549 sunflower (B) (4)
▨ Tunisian size L and N crochet hooks *or sizes to obtain gauge*
▨ Yarn needle

GAUGES

▨ 11 sts and 8 rows to 4"/10cm over Tunisian st using size N crochet hook and 2 strands MC tog.
▨ 9 sts and 8 rows to 3"/7.5cm over Tunisian st using size L crochet hook and 1 strand B.
Take time to check gauges.

Notes

1 Small stars are worked separately and then appliquéd.

2 To start a new color, drop old color behind work and draw up lp in next st leaving tail in back of work. Continue drawing up lps of new color until next color change or the end of the row.

3 To pick up a previously used color, cross yarns to prevent gapping by pulling old color to the left and across the back of the next stitch. Draw up new color over the old, locking old color in place, and draw new color through 2 lps on the hook. Let old color drop to back of work.

STITCH GLOSSARY

Tunisian Simple St

Each row is worked in two passes—the forward pass and the reverse pass. All rows are worked from the RS.

1 Base Row In 2nd ch from hook, draw lp and leave on hook, *draw lp in next ch and leave on hook; rep from * across. Do not turn.

2 Reverse Yo and draw through first lp, *yo and draw through 2 lps; rep from * to end of row until 1 lp rem.

3 Forward *Draw lp from under vertical bar from right to left and leave on hook; rep from * across. Do not turn.

Rep steps 2 and 3 for each row, ending with step 2.

BLANKET

With 2 strands MC and larger hook, ch 71.
Rows 1–55 Follow chart and work in Tunisian st. Each chart square = 1 st.

FACES

With B and smaller hook, ch 11 and following chart and make 1 large face. With B and smaller hook, ch 6 and following chart make 2 small faces.

APPLIQUÉD STARS

(make 4)
Rnd 1 With 2 strands A and smaller hook, ch 1, 5 sc into ch. Join with sl st to first sc.
Rnd 2 Ch 2, 2 sc into each sc. Join with sl st to first sc—10 sc.
Rnd 3 [Ch 6, sl st in 2nd ch from hook, 1 sc in next ch, 1 hdc in next ch, 1 dc in each of last 2 ch. Skip 1 sc on rnd 2, sl st in next sc] 5 times. Fasten off.

BORDER

Join 2 strands B to edge of blanket.
Rnd 1 With larger hook, ch 3 (counts as 1 dc), 1 dc in each st around blanket, 5 dc in each corner. Join with sl st to top of beg ch-3—258 dc.
Rnd 2 Ch 3, 1 hdc in each dc, 5 dc in center dc of corner cluster. Join with sl st to top of beg ch-3—266 hdc. Fasten off.

FINISHING

Weave in ends. Stitch appliquéd stars to blanket. With 2 strands B, sew faces to top of stars. Block.

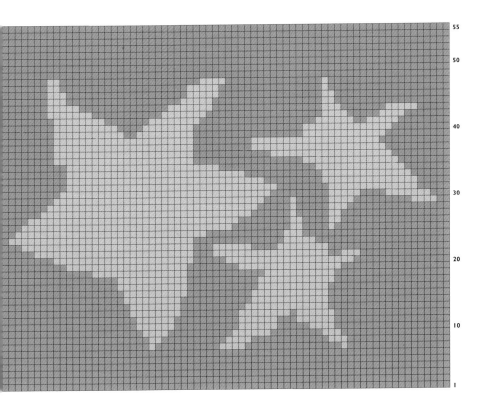

Color Key

- Gray
- Yellow
- Blue

TRADITIONAL GRANNY BLANKET

Petunia patchwork

Colorful granny squares are combined along with a 5-row border edging of clusters and picot. Designed by Margarita Mejia.

FINISHED MEASUREMENTS

■ 25"/63.5cm wide x 28"/71cm long

MATERIALS

■ 3 2.5oz/70g skeins (each approx 168yds/154m) of Lion Brand Yarn *Microspun* (microfiber acrylic) in #124 mocha (MC) **3**

■ 2 skeins each in #186 mango (A), #146 fuchsia (B) and #98 vanilla (D)

■ 1 skein in #103 coral (C)

■ Size E/4 (3.5mm) crochet hook *or size to obtain gauge*

■ Yarn needle

GAUGE

Each square approx 3" x 3"/7.5cm x 7.5cm using size E/4 (3.50mm) crochet hook. *Take time to check gauge.*

STITCH GLOSSARY

Cluster (CL) 3 Dc in same ch sp or st.

GRANNY SQUARE

(make 56)

Note See placement diagram for color order of first 3 rnds.

With first color, ch 4. Join with sl st to form ring.

Rnd 1 (RS) Ch 5 (counts as 1 dc and ch 2), [1 dc in ring, ch 2] 7 times. Join with sl st to 3rd ch of beg ch-5. Fasten off.

Rnd 2 Join 2nd color with sl st in any ch-2 sp. Ch 3 (counts as 1 dc), (2 dc in same sp, ch 2), [3 dc in next ch-2 sp, ch 2] 7 times. Join with sl st to 3rd ch of beg ch-5. Fasten off.

Rnd 3 Join 3rd color with sl st in any ch-2 sp. Ch 3 (counts as 1 dc), (2 dc, ch 1, 3 dc) in same sp, ch 1, [(3 dc, ch 1, 3 dc) in next ch-2 sp, ch 1] 7 times. Join with sl st to 3rd ch of beg ch-5. Fasten off.

Rnd 4 Join MC with sl st in any ch-1 sp. Ch 3 (counts as 1 dc), (2 dc, ch 1, 3 dc) in same sp—first corner made, ch 1, *[1 sc in next ch-1 sp, ch 2] twice, 1 sc in next ch-1 sp, ch 1, (3 dc, ch 1, 3 dc) in next ch-1 sp for corner, ch 1; rep from * around, ending last rep with [1 sc in next ch-1 sp, ch 2] twice, sc in next ch-1 sp, ch 1. Join with sl st to 3rd ch of beg ch-5. Fasten off.

FINISHING

Arrange squares foll placement diagram for colorways and join together.

EDGING

Note On rnd 1, in addition to working into the 4 outer corner ch-1 sps of corner squares to form new corners, work across each side edge of the blanket and into the inner corner ch-1 sps of squares at the joined seams.

Rnd 1 (RS) Join MC with sl st in any outer corner ch-1 sp. Ch 5 (counts as 1 hdc and ch 3), 1 hdc in same sp— first corner made, **ch 2, *1 hdc in next ch-1 sp, ch 2, [1 hdc in next ch-2 sp, ch 2] twice, 1 hdc in next ch-1 sp, ch 2, 1 hdc in opposite corner ch-1 sp of same square, ch 2, skip joined seam, 1 hdc in corner ch-1 sp of next square, ch 2; rep from * to next outer corner ch-1 sp, (1 hdc, ch 3, 1 hdc) in sp; rep from ** around. Join with sl st to 2nd ch of beg ch-5. Fasten off.

Rnd 2 Join A with sl st in any corner ch-3 sp. Ch 3 (counts as 1 dc), 4 dc in same sp – first corner made, ch 2, *CL in next ch-2 sp, ch 2, skip next ch-2 sp; rep from * to next corner ch-3 sp, 5 dc in sp, ch 2; rep from * around, ending last rep with CL in next ch-2 sp, ch 2. Join with sl st to top of beg ch-3. Fasten off.

Rnd 3 Join C with sl st in first dc of any 5-dc corner. Ch 3 (counts as 1 dc), 2 dc in same st, ch 1, 5 dc in 3rd dc of same corner, ch 1, work CL in 5th dc of same corner, ch 2, *CL in 2nd dc of next CL, ch 2; rep from * to next 5-dc corner, (CL in first dc of corner, ch 1, 5 dc in 3rd dc, ch 1, CL in 5th dc) ch 2; rep from * around, ending last rep with CL in 2nd dc of next CL, ch 2. Join with sl st to 3rd ch of beg ch-3. Fasten off.

Rnd 4 Join B with sl st in first dc of any 5-dc corner. Ch 3 (counts as 1 dc), 2 dc in same st, ch 1, 5 dc in 3rd dc of same corner, ch 1, work CL in 5th dc of same corner, ch 2, *CL in 2nd dc of next CL, ch 2; rep from * to next 5-dc corner, (CL in first dc of corner, ch 1, CL in 3rd dc, ch 1, CL in 5th dc) ch 2; rep from * around, ending last rep with CL in 2nd dc of next CL, ch 2. Join with sl st to 3rd ch of beg ch-3. Fasten off.

Rnd 5 Join D with sl st in 2nd dc of any corner CL. Ch 7 (counts as 1 dc and ch 4), sl st in 4th ch from hook—Picot made, 1 dc in same st, ch 2, *1 sc in next ch-sp, 1 dc in 2nd dc of next cluster, ch 4, sl st in 4th ch from hook, 1 dc in same st, ch 2; rep from * around. Join with sl st to 3rd ch of beg ch-7. Fasten off.

C, B, A	A, C, B	D, A, C	B, MC, A	D, MC, B	C, B, A	B, MC, B	A, D, A
MC, C, B	C, A, D	B, MC, A	C, A, B	C, D, A	MC, D, C	A, D, A	MC, C, B
B, MC, A	MC, D, B	C, A, D	B, MC, A	C, B, D	D, A, B	B, MC, D	C, B, A
C, A, D	D, A, C	A, C, B	MC, D, C	D, MC, B	B, C, A	MC, C, B	B, A, C
D, A, B	B, MC, A	C, A, D	D, A, B	A, C, A	MC, D, B	C, D, A	D, B, D
MC, D, C	A, B, D	MC, D, B	A, B, A	MC, C, B	C, B, A	MC, D, C	B, MC, A
B, C, A	D, MC, B	B, C, A	C, B, D	D, A, C	MC, D, B	C, B, A	A, C, D

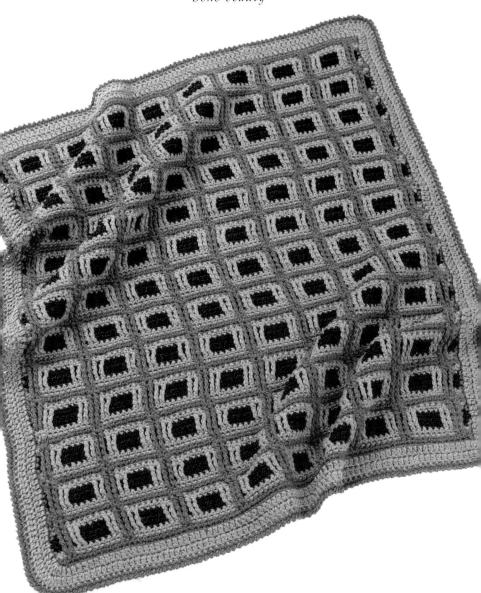

■■■▭

Neutral colors meet texture in this contemporary blanket design by Linda Medina. Double and quadruple trebles create geometric relief in a single crochet background.

FINISHED MEASUREMENTS
■ 28"/71cm wide x 31"/79cm long

MATERIALS
■ 4 3.5oz/100g skeins (each approx 250yds/229m) of South West Trading Company *Bamboo* (bamboo) in chocolate (MC) (4)
■ 3 skeins jade (A)
■ 3 skeins navy (B)
■ Size H/8 (5mm) crochet hook *or size to obtain gauge*
■ Yarn needle

GAUGE
14 sts and 19 rows to 4"/10cm over treble pat using size H/8 (5mm) crochet hook. *Take time to check gauge.*

Notes
1 Use 2 strands of yarn held tog throughout unless otherwise indicated.

2 Join new color at end of row, working st in old color to last 2 lps; leaving 6"/15cm tail, complete st by drawing new color through 2 lps and continue with new color.

STITCH GLOSSARY
Double Treble Relief Front (Dtr/rf) Yo 3 times, insert hook from front to back to front around next sc 5 rows below present row, yo and draw lp (5 loops on hook), [yo and draw through 2 lps] 4 times.

Quadruple Treble Relief Front (Quadtr/rf) Yo 5 times, insert hook from front to back to front around next sc 9 rows below present row, yo and draw loop, (7 lps on hook), [yo and draw through 2 lps] 6 times.

BLANKET
With A, ch 85.

Row 1 (RS) 1 Sc in 2nd ch from hook and in each ch across—84 sc. Turn.

Row 2 Ch 1, 1 sc in each sc across. Turn.

Rows 3 and 4 With MC, rep row 2. Turn.

Rows 5–8 With B, rep row 2. Turn.

Row 9 With MC, ch 1, 1 sc in first 3 sc, *[Dtr/rf] twice, 1 sc in each of next 4 sc, [Dtr/rf] twice, 1 sc in each of next 2 sc; rep from * across, ending with 1 sc in last sc. Turn.

Row 10 Ch 1, 1 sc in each sc across. (For Dtr/rf sts, work st through the top of the sc from 2 rows below and Dtr/rf tog.) Turn.

Row 11 With A, ch 1, 1 sc in first sc. *[Quadtr/rf] twice, 1 sc in each of next 8 sc; rep from * across, ending last rep with

[Quadtr/rf] twice, 1 sc in last sc. Turn.

Row 12 Ch 1, 1 sc in each sc across. (For Quadtr/rf sts, work st through the top of the sc from 2 rows below and Quadtr/rf tog.) Turn.

Rows 13–132 Rep rows 3–12, 12 times.

Row 133 With A, rep row 2. Fasten off.

SIDE EDGINGS

Attach A with sl st at corner along one long side of blanket. Work 1 row of sc along side edge. Fasten off. Rep for opp side edge.

BORDER

Beg at top right edge corner, skip 1 sc for corner, attach MC with sl st in next sc.

Rnd 1 (RS) Ch 3 (counts as 1 dc), *1 dc in each sc across to last sc, 4 dc in sc for corner; rep from * around, ending with 4 dc in first sc of top edge. Join with sl st to top of beg ch-3.

Rnd 2 Ch 3, (counts as 1 dc), 1 dc in each dc around, 4 dc in each corner. Join with sl st to top of beg ch-3. Fasten off.

Rnd 3 With A, ch 1, 1 sc in each dc around. Join with sl st to first sc. Fasten off one strand of A.

Rnd 4 With one strand A, ch 1, working from left to right, 1 sc in last st of previous row and in each st across. Join with sl st to first sc. Fasten off.

FINISHING

Weave in ends. Block lightly.

EYELET BLANKET

Lilac luxe

An iris pattern of V stitches comes together to make lace in this design by Walonika Emele. Contrast shell edging finishes the lace piece.

FINISHED MEASUREMENTS

■ 25"/63.5cm wide x 31"/79cm long

MATERIALS

■ 5 1.75oz/50g skeins (each approx 125yds/114m) of Plymouth Yarn *Royal Cashmere* (cashmere) in #828N light purple (MC) 🔵

■ 1 skein in #100Z magenta (CC)

■ Size H/8 (5mm) crochet hook *or size to obtain gauge*

■ Yarn needle

GAUGE

16 sts and 8 rows to 4"/10cm over iris st pat using size H/8 (5mm) crochet hook. *Take time to check gauge.*

BLANKET

With MC, ch 95.

Row 1 (2 Dc, ch 1, 2 dc) in 5th ch from hook, *skip 3 ch, (2 dc, ch 1, 2 dc) in next ch; rep from * to last 2 ch, skip 1 ch, 1 dc in last ch. Turn.

Row 2 Ch 3, skip first 3 dc, *(2 dc, ch 1, 2 dc) in ch-1 sp, skip next 4 dc; rep from * ending with skip last 2 dc, 1 dc in last ch. Turn.

Rep row 2 until piece measures 29"/73.5cm from beg. Fasten off.

EDGING

Rnd 1 (RS) With CC, ch 1, 1 sc in each st or space around blanket. Join with sl st to beg ch-1. Turn.

Rnd 2 Ch 1, skip first sc, 1 sc in each sc around. Join with 1 sc to beg ch-1. Turn.

Rnd 3 Ch 1, skip first sc, *skip 1 sc, 5 dc in next sc, skip 1 sc, 1 sc in next sc; rep from * around. Join with 1 sc to beg ch-1. Fasten off.

FINISHING

Weave in ends.

This blanket features 3-D flower grannies, filet grannies, and diagonal stripes on the increase and decrease, along with horizontal striped blocks. Designed by Simona Merchant-Dest.

FINISHED MEASUREMENTS

■ 32"/81.5cm wide x 38"/96.5cm long

MATERIALS

■ 6 1.75oz/50g skeins (each approx 108yds/99m) of Tahki Yarns/Tahki•Stacy Charles, Inc. *Cotton Classic* (mercerized cotton) in #3447 dusty rose (A) ■ 4 ■

■ 5 skeins each in #3003 ecru (B) and #3712 sage (C)

■ Yarn needle

■ Size F/5 (3.75mm) crochet hook *or size to obtain gauge*

GAUGE

Each square approx 5½"/14.6cm x 5½"/14.6cm using size F/5 (3.75mm) crochet hook.

Take time to check gauge.

Notes

1 Rose and ecru with rose squares are worked in rounds.

2 Horizontal 3-stripe and diagonal stripe squares are worked in rows.

3 Join new color at end of row by working st in old color to last 2 lps; leaving 6"/15cm tail, complete st by drawing new color through 2 lps and continue with new color.

STITCH GLOSSARY

Treble (tr) Yo twice and draw lp (4 lps on hook), [yo and draw through 2 lps] 3 times.
Double Treble (dtr) Yo 3 times and draw lp (5 lps on hook), [yo and draw through 2 lps] 4 times.

ROSE SQUARE

(make 8)

With A, ch 6. Join with sl st to form ring.
Rnd 1 Ch 3 (counts as 1 dc), 2 dc in ring, *ch 3, 3 dc in ring; rep from* twice more, ch 2. Join with 1 sc in top of the beg ch-3.
Rnd 2 Ch 3 (counts as 1 dc), 2 dc in sc, *1 dc in each of next 3 dc, (3 dc, ch 3, 3 dc) in ch-3 corner sp; rep from * twice more, 1 dc in each of next 3 dc, (3 dc, ch 2) in ch-3 corner sp. Join with 1 sc in top of beg ch-3.
Rnd 3 Ch 3 (counts as 1 dc), 2 dc in sc, *1 dc in each of next 9 dc, (3 dc, ch 3, 3 dc) in ch-3 corner sp; rep from * twice more, 1 dc in each of next 9 dc, (3 dc, ch 2) in ch-3 corner sp. Join with 1 sc in top of beg ch-3.
Rnd 4 Ch 3 (counts as 1 dc), 2 dc in sc, *1 dc in each of next 15 dc, (3 dc, ch 3, 3 dc) in ch-3 corner space; rep from * twice more, 1 dc in each of next 15 dc, (3 dc, ch 2) in ch-3 corner sp. Join with 1 sc in top of beg ch-3.
Rnd 5 Ch 3 (counts as 1 dc), 2 dc in sc, *[ch 2, skip 3 dc, 1 dc in each of next 3 dc] 3 times, ch 2, skip 3 dc, (3 dc, ch 3, 3 dc) in

ch-3 corner sp; rep from * twice more, [ch 2, skip 3 dc, 1 dc in each of next dc] 3 times, ch 2, skip 3 dc, (3 dc, ch 2) in ch-3 corner sp. Join with 1 sc in top of beg ch-3.

Rnd 6 Ch 3 (counts as 1 dc), 2 dc in sc, *skip 1 dc, then work [1 dc in each of next 3 dc, 2 dc in ch-2 sp] 4 times, 1 dc in each of next 2 dc, (3 dc, ch 3, 3 dc) in ch-3 corner sp; rep from * twice more, skip 1 dc, [1 dc in each of next 3 dc, 2 dc in ch-2 sp] 4 times, 1 dc in each of next 2 dc, (3 dc, ch 2) in ch-3 corner sp. Join with 1 sc to top of beg ch-3. Fasten off.

ECRU SQUARE WITH ROSE FLOWER
(make 8)
Base Square
With B, ch 6. Join with sl st to form ring. Rep rnds 1–6 of Pink Square.
Rose Flower
Chain Circle With A, sl st through center ch-6 ring of white square in sp between 3-dc groups, ch 2, *1 sc in next sp between 3-dc group of white square center ring, ch1; rep from * twice more. Join with sl st to first ch beg ch-2—8 sts.

Rnd 1 Ch 1,*1 sc in each of next 3 sts, 2 sc in next st; rep from * once more. Join with sl st to first sc—10 sts.

Rnd 2 Ch 2 (counts as 1 hdc), 1 hdc in same place, *2 hdc in each sc; rep from * 8 times more. Join with sl st to top of beg ch-2—20 sts.

Rnd 3 Working in FL of each st, *ch 3, 1 trc in same place, 2 trc in each of next 2 hdc, (1 trc, ch 3, sl st) in next hdc, sl st in next hdc; rep from * 4 times more.

Rnd 4 Working in BL of each st, sl st into first st, ch 2, * 1 hdc in each of first 4 hdc from rnd 2, 2 hdc in next hdc; rep from * 3 times more. Join with sl st – 24 sts..

Rnd 5 Ch 4, 1 dtr in same place, 2 dtr in each of next 2 hdc, (1 dtr, ch 4, sl st 1) in next hdc, sl st in next hdc; rep from * 5 times more. Fasten off.

Rnd 6 With B, sl st around post of sc of rnd 1, *ch 5, skip 1 sc, sl st around post of 2nd sc of rnd 1; rep from * 4 times more. Join with sl st. Fasten off.

3-STRIPES SQUARE
(make 7)
With C, ch 29.
Row 1 1 Dc in 3rd ch from hook, 1 dc in each ch across. Turn.

Rows 2, 4, 6 Ch 1, 1 sc in each st across. Turn.

Rows 3, 5 Ch 3 (counts as 1 dc), 1 dc in each st across. Fasten off. Join A.
With A, rep rows 1–6. Fasten off. Join B.
With B, rep rows 1–6. Fasten off.

DIAGONAL STRIPES SQUARE
(make 7)
With C, ch 2.
Row 1 1 Sc in 2nd ch from hook. Turn.
Row 2 Ch 1, 3 sc in sc. Turn

Row 3 Ch 1, 2 sc in first sc (inc made), 1 sc in next sc, 2 sc in last sc (inc made). Turn.

Row 4 Ch 1, 2 sc in 1st sc (inc made), 1 sc in each of next 3 sc, 2 sc in last sc (inc made). Fasten off. Turn.

Cont in pat as established working sc across all rows and incs at beg and end of rows.

Rows 5 and 7 With A, ch 1, 2 sc in first sc (inc made), 1 sc in each sc, 2 sc in last sc (inc made). Turn.

Rows 6 and 8 Ch 1, 1 sc in each sc. Turn.

Rows 9–11 With B, rep row 5.

Row 12 Rep row 6.

Rows 13 and 14 With C, rep rows 5 and 6.

Rows 15 and 16 Rep row 5.

Rows 17 and 18 With A, rep rows 5 and 6.

Rows 19 and 20 With B, rep rows 5 and 6.

Rows 21 and 22 With C, rep row 5.

Rows 23 and 24 With A, rep rows 5 and 6.

Row 25 Rep row 5—35 sc.

Row 26 (Dec) Ch 1, skip first sc, 1 sc in each sc across to last 2 sc, skip 1 sc, 1 sc in last sc. Turn.

Row 27 With B, ch 1, 1 sc in each sc across. Turn.

Row 28 Rep row 26.

Rows 29 and 30 With C, rep row 26.

Rows 31 and 32 With A, rep rows 27 and 28.

Row 33 With B, rep row 27.

Rows 34–36 Rep row 26.

Rows 37 and 38 With C, rep rows 27 and 28.

Rows 39 and 40 With A, rep rows 27 and 28.

Rows 41 and 42 With B, rep row 26.

Rows 43 and 44 With C, rep rows 27 and 28.

Rows 45 and 46 Rep rows row 28.

Rows 47 and 48 With A, rep row 28.

Row 49 Skip first sc, 1 sc in next sc, sl st in next sc. Fasten off.

FINISHING

Block Edging

Sl st in any corner, *3 sc in corner, 24 sc along side of squares; rep from * 3 times more. Join with sl st to first sc. Fasten off. Block squares to measurements. Follow diagram layout and arrange blocks. With C, whipstitch squares tog working through back lps.

BORDER

Rnd 1 With C, sl st in one corner, (ch 3, 1 trc, ch 1, 2 dc) in corner, *1 dc in each st along side of blanket to corner st, (2 dc, ch 1, 2 tr, ch 1, 2 dc) in corner; rep from * twice more, ending with 1 dc in each st along last side to beg corner, (2 dc, ch 2) in corner. Join with sl st to top of beg ch-3.

Rnd 2 Ch 2, (1 tr, 1 dc, ch 1) in corner, * 1 dc in each st along side of blanket to corner st, (ch 1, 1 dc, 1 tr, 1 dc, ch 1) in corner; rep from * twice more, ending with 1 dc in each st along last side to beg corner, ch 1. Join with sl st to join to top of beg ch-2. Fasten off. Weave in ends.

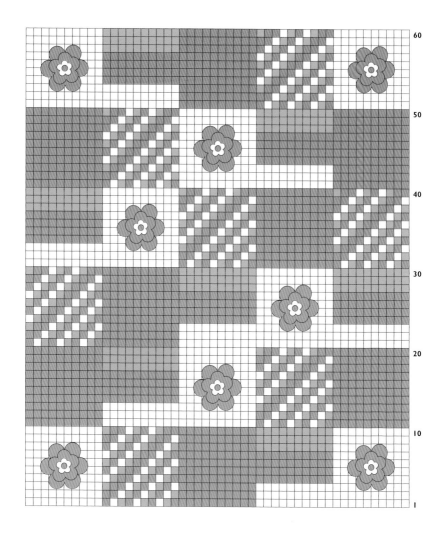

CABLED BLANKET

Orange you sleepy?

■ ■ ■ ▶

Designed by Mary Kathryn Simon, crossed double treble crochet stitches create columns of beautiful cables. Front and back post double treble stitch divides the columned cables, giving the blanket added dimension.

FINISHED MEASUREMENTS

■ 25"/63.5cm wide x 22"/60cm long

MATERIALS

■ 6 4oz/113g skeins (each approx 335yds/306m) of TLC/Coats & Clark *Cotton Plus* (acrylic) in #3252 tangerine 🄬
■ Size E/4 (3.5mm) crochet hook *or size to obtain gauge*
■ Yarn needle

GAUGE

20 sts and 9 rows to 4"/10cm over cable pat using size E/4 (3.5mm) crochet hook. *Take time to check gauge.*

Note When working on WS of blanket, be careful when working in front of last 3 dtrs to not to catch them with crochet hook; rather work 1 dtr into each of 3 sts just skipped.

STITCH GLOSSARY

Double Treble (dtr) Yo 3 times and draw lp in next stitch (5 lps on hook), [yo and draw through 2 lps] 4 times.

Treble Relief Front (Tr/rf) Yo twice, insert hook from front to back to front around post of st, yo and draw lp (4 loops on hook), [yo and draw through 2 lps] 3 times.

Treble Relief Back (Tr/rb) Yo twice, insert hook from back to front to back around post of st, yo and draw lp (4 loops on hook), [yo and draw through 2 lps] 3 times.

BLANKET

Ch 132.

Row 1 (WS) 1 Dc in 4th ch from hook, 1 dc in each ch across—129 dc. Turn.

Row 2 (RS) Ch 3 (counts as 1 dc), Tr/rf around next st, 1 dc in next st, *(skip 3 sts, 1 dtr in each of next 3 sts, working behind last 3 dtrs, 1 dtr into each 3 skipped st), 1 dc in next st, Tr/rf around next st, 1 dc in next st, (skip 3 sts, 1 dtr in each of next 3 sts, working in front of last 3 dtrs, 1 dtr into each 3 skipped st), 1 dc in next st, Tr/rf around next st, 1 dc in next st; rep from * to last 3 sts, ending with 1 dc in next st, Tr/rf around next st, 1 dc in last st. Turn.

Row 3 Ch 3 (counts as 1 dc), Tr/rb around next st, 1 dc in next st, *(skip 3 sts, 1 dtr in each of next 3 sts, working behind last 3 dtrs, 1 dtr into each 3 skipped st), 1 dc in next st, Tr/rb around next st, 1 dc in next st, (skip 3 sts, 1 dtr in each of next 3 sts, working in front of last 3 dtrs, 1 dtr into each 3 skipped st), 1 dc in next st, Tr/rb around next st, 1 dc in next st; rep from * to last 3 sts, ending with 1 dc in next st, Tr/rb around next st, 1 dc in last st. Turn.

Rep rows 2 and 3 until work meas approx 22"/60cm. Fasten off.

Weave in ends.

RESOURCES

U.S. RESOURCES

Write to the yarn companies listed below for purchasing and mail-order information.

Alchemy Yarns of Transformation
P.O. Box 1080
Sebastopol, CA 95473
www.alchemyyarns.com

Artyarns, Inc.
39 Westmoreland Avenue
White Plains, NY 10606
www.artyarns.com

Blue Sky Alpacas
PO Box 387
St. Francis, MN 55070
www.blueskyalpacas.com

Caron International
200 West 3rd Street
Washington, NC 27889
www.caron.com

Classic Elite Yarns
122 Western Avenue
Lowell, MA 01851
www.classiceliteyarns.com

Coats & Clark
3430 Toringdon Way,
Suite 301
Charlotte, NC 28277
www.coatsandclark.com

Fiesta Yarns
5401 San Diego NE
Albuquerque, NM 87112
www.fiestayarns.com

Filatura Di Crosa
distributed by
Tahki•Stacy Charles, Inc.

GGH
distributed by
Muench Yarns

Karabella Yarns
1201 Broadway
New York, NY 10001
www.karabellayarns.com

Lion Brand Yarn
34 West 15th Street
New York, NY 10011
www.lionbrand.com

Lorna's Laces
4229 North Honore Street
Chicago, IL 60613
www.lornaslaces.net

Mission Falls
100 Walnut, Door 4
Champlain, NY 12919
www.missionfalls.com

Muench Yarns, Inc.
1323 Scott Street
Petaluma, CA 94954-1135
www.myyarns.com

Nashua Handknits
distributed by
Westminster Fibers, Inc.

Plymouth Yarn Company
P.O. Box 28
Bristol, PA 19007
www.plymouthyarn.com

Red Heart
distributed by
Coats & Clark

Rowan Yarns
distributed by
Westminster Fibers, Inc.

South West Trading Company
918 South Park Lane,
Suite 102
Tempe, AZ 85281
www.soysilk.com

Tahki•Stacy Charles, Inc.
70-30 80th Street
Building #36
Ridgewood, NY 11385
www.tahkistacycharles.com

Tahki Yarns
distributed by
Tahki•Stacy Charles, Inc.

TLC
distributed by
Coats & Clark

Westminster Fibers
4 Townsend West, Unit 8
Nashua, NH 03063
www.westminsterfibers.com

CANADIAN RESOURCES

Write to U.S. resources for mail-order availability of yarns not listed.

Bernat
320 Livingstone Avenue
South
Listowel, Ontario
Canada N4W 3H3
www.bernat.com

Koigu Wool Designs
Box 158
563295 Glenelg Holland
Townline
Chatsworth, Ontario
Canada NOH 1G0
www.koigu.com

Mission Falls
5333 Casgrain, #1204
Montreal, Quebec
Canada H2T 1X3
www.missionfalls.com

S.R. Kertzer, Ltd.
50 Trowers Road
Woodbridge, ON
Canada L4L 7K6
www.kertzer.com

U.K. RESOURCES

Not all yarns used in this book are available in the U.K. For yarns not available, make a comparable substitute or contact the U.S. manufacturer for purchasing and mail-order information.

Rowan
Green Lane Mill
Holmfirth
HD9 2DX England
www.knitrowan.com

VOGUE® KNITTING CROCHETED BABY BLANKETS

Vice President,
Publisher
TRISHA MALCOLM

Editorial Director
ELAINE SILVERSTEIN

Art Director
CHI LING MOY

Executive Editor
CARLA S. SCOTT

Book Division Manager
ERICA SMITH

Graphic Designer
SHEENA T. PAUL

Associate Editor
ERIN WALSH

Yarn Editor
TANIS GRAY

Instructions Editor
JEANNIE CHIN

Instructions Proofreader
RITA GREENFEDER

Production Manager
DAVID JOINNIDES

Photography
JACK DEUTSCH STUDIO

Photo Stylist
LAURA MAFFEO

Copy Editor
KRISTINA SIGLER

President,
Sixth&Spring Books
ART JOINNIDES

LOOK FOR THESE OTHER TITLES IN THE *VOGUE KNITTING ON THE GO!* SERIES…